BOB SMEATON

FROM BENWELL BOY TO 46TH BEATLE… AND BEYOND

A Memoir

Second edition published in 2019 by Heddon Publishing.
First published in 2018.

ISBN 978-1-9995963-3-0

Cover design by Catherine Clarke

Back cover image courtesy of McVirn Etienne

This book is dedicated to John Benson and Chips Chipperfield,
true music men.

THE 46TH BEATLE

MADISON SQUARE GARDEN, NEW YORK
26TH FEBRUARY 1997

"It's a long way from Newcastle in the North of England to Madison Square Garden in New York. I would like to thank John, Paul, George and Ringo for making this journey possible."

As I looked out across the vast arena – packed with fifteen thousand people - and made my Grammy acceptance speech, I realised this was as close as I would ever get to performing on this hallowed stage. Frank Sinatra, Elvis, the Rolling Stones and Jimi Hendrix had all stood in this very spot, looking out at a sea of people, as I was doing now.

I had dreamt that one day I would perform with my band White Heat in this place. Just its name had a magical ring to it; Madison Square Garden. I remembered, as a kid, being sat in front of a black and white TV watching Muhammad Ali box here and as an eighteen-year-old I had queued to see Led Zeppelin's movie *The Song Remains the Same*, which had been filmed here.

It was on a cold December morning back in 1991, standing on a platform at Newcastle Central train station, that my friend Geoff Wonfor offered me the chance to work alongside him on a documentary about 'the most famous group of all time'. I could never have imagined that six years later I would be picking up a Grammy. If my life had ended on that night, I would have died a happy man. I felt like I had reached the top of a mountain.

I had spent the previous five years as series director and writer on *The Beatles Anthology*. The first episode aired on ABC television in America on 19th November 1995, to an audience of 47 million. It was broadcast a week later on ITV in the UK, and around the rest of the world. The series ran for six hours; it was the first time that a documentary of this size and scope had ever been made about one group and it would set the benchmark for every music documentary that followed.

I would be lying if I said that, when I first seriously started getting into music during my early teens, the Beatles were my favourite group; they didn't even come close. They didn't have a guitar player who could hammer out riffs like Jimmy Page from Led Zeppelin or a lead singer who could scream like Roger Daltrey from the Who, and there was no front man to rival Mick Jagger. I had never bought a Beatles record on the day it was released; in fact, the only Beatles album I owned was the *Red* half of the *Red and Blue* greatest hits compilation. I do not even recall paying much attention when the news broke in the early 1970s that they were splitting up; I would have been thirteen at the time and there were more important things happening in my life.

But, while the Beatles might not have been my favourite group, they had been a presence in my life since I was a kid. When I was seven years old, my mam had taken me to see their second feature film, *Help*, at the Odeon cinema in Newcastle. I remember walking backwards up the aisle as the end credits rolled, not wanting to miss a single frame. A couple of years later, while babysitting my sister Suzanne, I would serenade her to sleep by singing the opening lines of *All My Loving*.

While working on the *Anthology* I had been able to find out first-hand from Ringo Starr why the band had decided to film part of *Help* in the Bahamas, and to ask Paul McCartney how he had come to write the song whose melody would send my baby sister off to sleep.

A couple of years into the job, George Harrison told me that one day I would write a book about the Beatles. He said that there were people who had written books about them who had never even been in the same room as one of them. In fact, it would never be my intention to write a book about the Beatles; there are thousands of those already, cluttering up the bookshelves of Beatles fans all over the world. But I did understand what George was saying. I was in a privileged position, helping the Beatles bring their story to the screen. Those five years I spent working on that series pretty much changed my life.

When we were working on the *Anthology*, Geoff, Andy Matthews (the editor) and I would often discuss who we felt was worthy of being called the 'fifth Beatle'.

George Martin, who produced all the group's recordings aside from their *Let It Be* album, would be many people's first choice.

Billy Preston, who had actually performed live with the Beatles during their final performance, on the roof of the Apple offices in Savile Row, would also be a contender.

My own vote would have been given to Neil Aspinall who, aside from being the executive producer on the *Anthology*, had worked for the Beatles almost all of his adult life; initially as a roadie, eventually becoming the head of Apple - the company that the Beatles had set up in the late 1960s. I pointed out to Andy and Geoff that as I had interviewed all three of the Beatles still alive at the time on film, probably as many times as anyone, and I was also the last person ever to interview the three of them collectively, I would at least be somewhere in the top fifty. We counted back through all of the people who would be in the queue in front of me and decided that I would probably be the 46th Beatle. I would happily settle for that.

BENWELL

ALL THE LADS AND LASSES THERE

For most of the first thirty years of my life, I lived in Benwell; an area in the West End of Newcastle where the streets ran down to Scotswood Road; immortalised in the chorus of the song *Blaydon Races*:

'All the lads and lasses there all with smiling faces
gannin alang the Scotswood Road to see the Blaydon Races.'

Hank Marvin, the guitarist in Cliff Richard's band the Shadows, also grew up around our way, as did Alan Hull from Lindisfarne. But the most famous person ever to come from Benwell was Willie Fisher.

Willie, like many working class kids - myself included - who were born within spitting distance of the banks of the River Tyne, would find work in the Swan Hunter Shipyards. Willie chose the 'white collar' route, becoming a draughtsman, while I went down the 'blue collar' route and became a welder.

Growing tired of life in the shipyards, Willie quit his job and moved to Russia, where he subsequently changed his name to Rudolf Abel and become a Russian spy. Rudolf was by all accounts a much better spy than Willie was a draughtsman. He was so good, in fact, that a Hollywood film has been made about his exploits. In 2015, he was portrayed by the actor Mark Rylance in Steven Spielberg's film *Bridge of Spies*.

Sting – who, before finding fame and fortune with his band the Police, had lived in Wallsend, not far from the shipyards – asked Mark Rylance if he would be playing Rudolf with the notoriously difficult to mimic Geordie accent. Mark was fantastic in the film, winning an Oscar for his performance, but had decided to play the role with a Scottish accent. That is what is called in the trade 'artistic license'.

None of this is to say that Willie (or Rudolf) and I were friends. In fact, during 1957 - the year that I was born - Willie was standing trial in America for conspiracy as a Russian spy. He was sentenced to thirty years' imprisonment.

That is how Willie Fisher became the most famous person ever to have been born in Benwell. But he never won a Grammy.

My dad was also born in Benwell and served his time in the shipyards but, rather than follow the Willie Fisher route out of 'the yards', he thought he would be able to punch his way out. He joined the Grainger Park Boys Club and subsequently became Northumberland All Boys Boxing Champion.

It was at an amateur boxing contest that he met my mam. Despite being a boxer, he was 'lovely looking' and by all accounts he had an eye for the girls. My mam told me that he could have had any girl he wanted but he wanted her; and he always got what he wanted. He had two older brothers, Billy and Jimmy, and two sisters, Connie and Dorothy. Dorothy was the youngest in the family but in their mother's eyes my dad was always the baby. He was idolised by her and he could do no wrong. That was until, at the age of seventeen, he announced that he had met a girl called Pauline Watson and they were going to get married.

Pauline Watson was the eldest in her family and had spent most of her teenage years babysitting her brothers, Arty and Chas. For her, getting married was as much about being able to live her own life as it was about marrying the 'best looking bloke in Benwell'.

On 22nd December 1956, less than a year after they began courting, Bob Smeaton and Pauline Watson got married. He was eighteen and she was twenty-two. My mam says that the reason my dad wanted to get married so quickly was that he was due to go off to do his National Service. He would be joining up as part of the Royal Army Medical Corps and stationed at Catterick Camp Barracks for two years. He was scared that she would meet somebody else while he was away.

Their first marital home was with my dad's mother; not the ideal situation for the newly-weds. However, to cement the deal, my dad thought it would also be a good idea to start a family and, once my mam fell pregnant, they were able to secure a one-bedroom, ground-floor, council flat.

A year to the month after they got married, my dad was given compassionate leave to return home to their flat at 43 Violet Street to meet his son, Bob Smeaton Junior. Then it was back to Catterick Camp. By the time he returned, his National Service complete, he had a one-year-old son who he hardly knew, and a wife he had spent very little time with. He gave up the boxing and went back to his job as a welder. He was twenty years old.

Being handy with his fists and spending time away from home were things which he never got out of his system, along with his eye for the girls.

***

Around the time I started South Benwell infant school, we were offered a two-bedroom house on a new council estate that had just been built in Westerhope. It was only four miles away from Benwell but for a six-year-old it might as well have been on the other side of the planet. I had loved South Benwell school. Most of the teachers were great, I had loads of friends, and I had also started playing for the school football team. I hated my new school; I felt like an alien, I couldn't make any friends, and I used to cry myself to sleep each night.

Thankfully, my mam was my salvation. Within two months of moving to Westerhope she decided she hated it, too, and after one massive 'shouting match' between her and my dad it was decided that we would move back. We were able to do an exchange for our house in Westerhope with a family who had a two-bedroom flat in Denton Gardens, Benwell. I was back with my old pals, at my old school. It was like I had never been away.

My mam and dad also slipped back into their old routine. Friday night was 'lads' night out', when my dad would go out with his mates, and Saturday was the night when they would go out together. My dad would scan the local paper, the *Evening Chronicle*, to find a social club that was holding a 'Go as You Please'. This was a chance for aspiring singers from the local area to show off their singing skills. Whoever the audience decided was the best would be rewarded with the prize of a joint of meat.

My dad had always fancied himself as a bit of a singer and I would often hear him singing along to his Frank Ifield records. Frank was an Australian singer who topped the UK charts a couple of times in the early 1960s. He had a peculiar yodelling style of singing that you might have expected of someone who hailed from Switzerland. What was even more surprising was that my dad made a pretty good fist of mimicking Frank's yodel. Had my dad been born fifty years later, he would have been appearing on the *X Factor*, but back then the best he could hope for would be winning the Go as You Please.

When my mam and dad arrived at a club, apparently word would go round that 'Bob Smeaton was in the house'. More often than not, my dad would come home on a Saturday night with a brown paper package under his arm. That would be us sorted for Sunday dinner.

What probably worked in my dad's favour was that, as well as being able to make a decent fist of the singing, he also looked the part. I recall once playing football in the street with a bunch of mates, early one summer evening, when he passed us on his way out to the Scotswood Social Club. He looked immaculate in his grey suit, white shirt and tie. One of my mates commented that he looked like the actor Tony Curtis while another said that when he grew up he hoped that he would be like my dad.

Whenever my mates came around to my house, my dad would chat to them about football, crack jokes, and always make them feel welcome. They would tell me how cool he was, how he was much younger than their dads. When I was in my mid-teens and started bringing girls back to the house, after they had left he would ask, "What did she think of me?" and, "How old did she think I looked?" I would lie and say they had said nothing. In fact, they would always remark about how handsome he was. He was good looking, funny, and all my mates thought he was great. I hated him.

Even though he had given up the boxing, my dad hadn't given up using his fists. He would hit me for the slightest reason. If I made a noise when I was eating my tea, or came in late from playing outside, he would whack me around the head. My mother would shout, "Not on the head, on the arse." He would grab me tightly by the arm and get right up into my face and shout at me. Just the sound of his voice was enough to make me shake with fear.

I would cower in the corner as his blows rained down on my head. When he did eventually stop, I would get back to my feet, literally seeing stars. I also remember a loud buzzing in my head. I would tell him that when I was older I would get my own back and beat him up. I never got to the point where I was big enough or brave enough to fight back. He was always bigger than me.

My mam was defenceless to do anything to stop him. If she did try to intervene, he would shout at her and tell her that she was too soft with me. She got her share of slaps, too. I remember once when they were having one their rows and she hid behind the door into the kitchen. Rather than open it, my dad punched a hole in the door, which almost connected with her on the other side. It would have been funny if it wasn't so scary.

Whenever he spoke to me or asked me a question, I was so scared of saying the wrong thing that I would stutter out my answer. He would mock me and ask me why I was stuttering. "What's wrong with you? Are you stupid or something?" It just made my stuttering worse. It got so bad that my mam decided to take me to see a speech therapist. We met a nice woman who sat me down for a chat. I didn't stutter. She gave me a book to read and I read a section without stuttering. It got to the point where I was feeling that I should stutter just so as not to disappoint her. The woman decided that the stuttering was not a physical thing, rather something that happened when I was scared or nervous.

I had thought maybe this was the kind of relationship most fathers had with their sons but, having been around to my friends' houses, I discovered this was not the case. I couldn't figure out why he behaved the way he did towards me. I was well-mannered, always said please and thank you, never got into any trouble, and was doing well at school. I was, as they used to say, a good lad. I even took up boxing for a short period of time and enrolled at the Grainger Park Boys Club. I thought that would win his approval but even that didn't seem to please him. Also, as much as I enjoyed the training, I didn't like being hit around the head. I didn't need to step into a boxing ring for that.

OUR TONY

My brother Tony was born on April Fool's Day 1961. It was a relief when he got to the age where he could take some of the heat off me. Whereas I was well-behaved and didn't feel like I deserved any of the beatings that came my way, 'our Tony' was always getting into trouble and was of the mind that the beatings came with the territory. Even before he was out of short trousers, he had a reputation. The local coppers, his teachers at school, and even the neighbours, had his card marked.

On one occasion, he and I paid a visit to the local Co-op supermarket; the first store in our area where goods could be paid for at the check-out rather than over the counter. What could be easier than picking something off a shelf and walking out without paying? I passed this information on to our Tony then walked around looking as innocent as possible, picked up a Mars Bar, stuffed it in my pocket and walked out of the door, my heart pounding.

A minute later, our Tony came running out with what looked like the contents of a Rowntree's factory stashed in his rolled-up jumper. He was already tucking into an Aztec. My laughter and my admiration for him were short-lived as he was followed round the corner by a very angry-looking shop assistant. We were both caught in the act. Luckily for us, the shop assistant knew my mam and frogmarched us to our house rather than calling the local police.

We sat in our kitchen with my mam and the lady from the shop, who were both judge and jury. On a promise that we would never steal again, it was decided that the police would not be called and that would be that. We both gave a sigh of relief that we had got away with it but our relief turned to terror when, just as the kind lady - who had surely saved us from what we thought was a stretch behind bars - was leaving, my dad came through the door.

We were both given 'the hiding of our lives'. The fact that our Tony had a much bigger haul than I did was not taken into consideration; it was deemed that, being his big brother, I should have known better than to coerce him into a potential life of crime.

From that day onwards, I never shoplifted again, but the thrashing that we were given did not totally deter my brother. Many years later, after we had both left school, a friend of mine asked me if our Tony had got a job working in Fenwick's department store in the centre of Newcastle. He had seen him walking out of the store wearing a white coat, pushing a fridge out on a trolley.

I had words with him but they fell on deaf ears. It wasn't until he got caught and spent some time at a probation centre for young offenders that he realised the error of his ways. But he never quite got rid of his crazy streak.

He now has the Tyne Bridge tattooed on a part of his anatomy where you should not have any tattoo, let alone one of Newcastle's most famous landmark. If you ever meet him, ask him to show you it; I am sure he will be happy to oblige. Just don't mention that I told you about it.

THE GEORDIE ELVIS

Fortunately for me, my dad started working on the oil rigs stationed off the shores of Aberdeen up in Scotland. He would be away from home for three weeks at a time, returning for two weeks before heading back. When he went offshore it would be a relief. I could breathe easy and eat my tea without fear of getting hit on the head. It also meant that I could raid his record collection.

Using the big brown radiogram, which had pride of place in our front room, I would play the same records again and again; what would now be called 'heavy rotation'. After every session, I had to make sure that each record was carefully put back into the correct sleeve, or there would be hell to pay when my dad got back. My mam was in on my secret but never uttered a word to him about what I was up to.

His record collection included the likes of Frank Ifield, Slim Whitman and Tom Jones but the greatest of all, to my untrained ears, was Elvis Presley. I had no idea at the time that Elvis had reshaped the world. To me, he was just another face on the sleeve of a single, and didn't look that different from Frank Ifield or Slim Whitman, aside from the fact that he had a great head of hair and didn't have a 'tache. I would like to be able to claim that it was *Heartbreak Hotel* or *Hound Dog* that first turned me on to 'the man who would be King' but in fact the record that got me dancing around our front room was *Do the Clam*. I had no idea what Elvis meant by 'doing the Clam' but whatever it was, he was really excited about it. When I eventually heard *Heartbreak Hotel* years later, I was a bit disappointed. I honestly thought that Elvis had blown it. He seemed as miserable as all hell; I must have only been around nine years old at the time and getting down to the 'bongo beat' while doing the Clam seemed a lot more fun than being at the end of a lonely street in a heartbreak hotel.

Green, Green Grass of Home by Tom Jones was another big favourite of mine. Not only did I love Tom's voice but the song told a great story. From what I could gather, the character in the song was returning to his home town after being away at an undisclosed destination. He is met by his family, who seem really pleased to see him, and he to see them. But all was not as it would appear; later in the song we discover that this happy return home has all been a dream. He is in fact just about to be hung, and buried beneath the 'green, green grass' of his hometown. Not really the sort of song that you would expect a ten-year-old to be into but beggars can't be choosers and until I could afford to buy my own records there was enough excitement within those grooves to fire my young imagination as I was singing along at the top of my voice.

Unlike my dad, I was never any good at copying the vocals of Frank Ifield or Slim Whitman. I could never quite grasp the yodelling style of singing but I always felt I was making a decent job on an Elvis or Tom Jones song. To this day I still know the words to Frank Ifield's *I Remember You*, and Slim Whitman's *Indian Love Call*. Put a song by Frank, Slim, Tom or Elvis on a karaoke machine and I will be up there singing along, without once having to look at the screen.

On Friday afternoons at South Benwell Junior School, we would have 'free time'. You could pretty much do whatever you wanted, aside from go home early. The artistic kids would put on plays or get up and sing songs, while the likes of me and my mates would head out into the schoolyard to play football. On one particular Friday, though, it was pissing down with rain, putting paid to any game of football. Instead, we decided to stay inside with the artistic kids.

We took our seats at the back of the class to watch those of our classmates who had the bottle to get up to perform. The audience would normally be appreciative of their efforts but on this occasion, with the addition of us lot, maybe less so. We basically took the piss out of anyone who had the audacity to get up and put on a performance. I remember the teacher asking, "Does anyone from our new additions want to get up and give us a song?"

Now at this point in time, the only singing I had done was in my front room at home. The thought of singing in front of an audience, especially one consisting of my mates, was a whole different ball game. But even though my guts were churning, I was desperate to get up and give it a go.

As I walked to the front of the class, I could hear my mates shouting, "Go on, Bob! The Geordie Elvis." I had decided to do my version of Tom Jones' *Delilah*. I knew all the words as my dad had recently added this song to his record collection. I really went for it and did all the actions in order to illustrate the story of the guy who comes home and catches his wife cheating on him with another man. He's so pissed off that when she starts laughing at him he feels a knife in his hand and 'she laughed no more'. I threw in a few Elvis moves for good measure and at the end of my rendition I was greeted with a round of applause from my mates. As I was walking back to join them, I noticed that a number of girls in the class were smiling at me. Maybe there was more to life than football.

MOVE ON UP

When my sister Suzanne was born in 1965, she quickly became the apple of my dad's eye. Having a girl in the house made him mellow a bit and there was a definite shift in our relationship. I still had to be on my guard for when the next slap on the head might come my way but for a couple of years they were coming less frequently. It even got to the point where we started going to 'the match' together.

We would go down to St James' Park to watch Newcastle United. My dad would put me in front of him, squeeze into the turnstile, and say, "One, please." He'd give the guy an extra couple of bob for letting me through. Occasionally, we would come up against a jobsworth who wouldn't let me in at the special 'reduced rate'. My dad would then have to pay full price, meaning no Bovril or pie at half-time. Once we were in the ground, he would sit me on the stone barrier, where I would have a clear view of the game. This was long before the stadiums became all-seated but my cold arse from sitting on the barrier was soon forgotten once the game kicked off. Those times we went to the game together are the happiest memories that I have of him.

We continued living in our two-bedroom flat on Denton Gardens but eventually we were offered a three-bedroom, newly-built council house just along the road, on Whickham View. This was the height of sophistication for us; just to be living in a house after living in flats for thirteen years was a giant leap forward. Our Tony and I would still be sharing a room but it offered enough space for us to split our bunk beds, putting paid to any arguments about who was going to draw the short straw and be on the top bunk. It also meant that our Sue would have her own room. And, for the first time ever, we would also have the luxury of a garden and an indoor toilet.

My dad even took up gardening for a while and would spend hours out there, tending to his chrysanthemums. The first thing he would do on his return home was look at how his garden was doing. When he wasn't in his garden, he would be doing bits of DIY around the house. He loved that house. He once built a fireplace, which he was really proud of, and he was always redecorating. One thing I would say about him was that he was hard-working.

My mam, on the other hand, would do as little work as possible. There would often be rows when my dad would get back from work and for his tea she had rustled up a Fray Bentos pie or a Vesta curry. She was a terrible cook, and most of what she did cook would come out of a packet or a tin. Often when I got back from school she would serve me up two packets of crisps and a KitKat. She still put them on a plate, to at least give the impression that I was getting a meal, and would tell me, "If your dad asks what you had for your tea, tell him that you had meat and vegetables." I didn't mind as I really loved crisps and KitKats. But my dad would protest that he wanted a cooked dinner. The deal as far as he was concerned was that he went out to work and she stayed at home, cooked the meals, and kept the house tidy. He kept to his side of the bargain but she was often left wanting in hers.

Moving to Whickham View also coincided with my changing schools from South Benwell Junior School to John Marley Senior School. John Marley was 'the big school' and very different to South Benwell. Just the fact that I would have to wear a school uniform was a big change in itself but the biggest change was that it was boys-only. To be at a school without any girls was unthinkable; also, there was no guarantee that I would be in the same class as any of my old pals. Being as it was the senior school meant that there would be kids coming from all over the West End of Newcastle. As the first day drew closer, I became more and more nervous at the thought of this new adventure that lay ahead of me.

My mam got herself into debt by getting a Provident Cheque which would be paid off monthly, in order to take me down to Farnons department store to make sure I had all the right stuff for my new school. On my first day I stood before her, in my dark-blue blazer, grey trousers and grey shirt. For the first time in my life I was wearing a tie, in the John Marley colours of maroon and gold. My mam was never one for any big show of emotions but seemed to be holding back a tear as she wished me good luck and told me not to let anyone pick on me, and to remember to stick up for myself.

Even before I started at John Marley, I was aware of the bitter rivalry between them and Slatyford School. The two hated each other for reasons that never became clear to me; maybe it was just because Slatyford was the nearest school to ours, or that they dressed in a school uniform of all black, giving them the appearance of being cooler. Regardless of the reasons, the fights between the two schools had become the stuff of legend. When they played each other at football, the ref blew the whistle to start the game and this would be a signal for the two teams to kick the shit out of each other. Who won at football was irrelevant; what mattered was who had the most players still standing at the end of ninety minutes.

Each school also had its own bus, in order to keep the two warring factions apart.

As I stood waiting for the number ten - the 'Marley Special' - on my first day, the 'Slaty Special' pulled up at the bus stop. Some of the Slatyford kids recognised my uniform and started spitting at me from an upstairs window. I replied by giving them two fingers. Someone must have thrown a brick out of the window; I felt a sharp pain above my eye and before I knew it I had blood streaming down the side of my face. I had the choice to go home and face the wrath of my mam, or arrive at school looking like I had just gone five rounds with Joe Bugner. I chose the latter.

I walked into the school yard and lined up with all the other kids. They must have thought I was really hard. Who was this kid who had turned up on his first day with blood pouring down his face? I got talking to some lads who had come from West Denton school, which had a reputation for churning out 'hard lads'. I told them that some kids from Slaty had attacked me with a brick but I had been able to fight them off. Even before the bell had rung, I had found some new mates.

TEENAGE KICKS

Within weeks of starting Marley, I became a member of the S.A.B. (Scotswood Aggro Boys). We were skinheads when being a 'skin' did not have the right-wing connotations that it does now. I adopted the moniker 'Bobbo' and would take great pleasure in spray-painting my name on the walls of the back lanes around Scotswood and Benwell. In an ideal world, I would have been walking the streets decked out in Doc Martens boots, a Ben Sherman shirt, and a pair of Levi Sta Prest trousers. Due to my lack of funds, I had to make do with a pair of my dad's old work boots, my grey school trousers hitched up over the top by a pair of braces, and a button-down-collared Brutus shirt (the next best thing to a Ben Sherman) that I had convinced my mam to buy me with the remaining proceeds of her 'Provy Cheque'. Being a skinhead coincided with my first becoming aware of the link between fashion and music. If you were a skinhead, you listened to Ska, although I didn't know that was what it was called at the time. *Skinhead Moonstomp* by Symarip and the *Double Barrel* by Dave and Ansel Collins were big favourites of ours but the greatest of them all was *The Liquidator* by the Harry J. All Stars. Despite being an instrumental, there was a part when a shout of 'skinheads' would be injected into the song. I loved it. This was a world away from Slim Whitman or Frank Ifield. This was our music.

I loved being part of a gang, too, and aside from having a mutual love of music and fashion, we were all reading the same book: *Skinhead* by Richard Allen. This was the first book that I ever willingly read from cover to cover. I am not sure if this was what would now be called 'classic literature' but I devoured every word on the page. The hero of the book, Joe Hawkins, was into exactly the same stuff as me and my mates: music, fashion, football, fighting, and girls.

During the weekends of the 'Summer of 1970', we would regularly catch the train from Newcastle Central Station to Whitley Bay and head to the Spanish City situated right on the seafront. This was the very same place that Mark Knopfler of Dire Straits would later name-check in the song *Tunnel of Love*, but I am sure Mark's memories of the place are very different to mine.

We would be there not to ride on the Tunnel of Love or to go crazy on the Waltzers but with the intention of looking for 'hairys'. Hairys were any blokes with long hair, or wearing flared trousers, who we viewed as the enemy. Pitched battles would be fought along the seafront 'from Cullercoats to Whitley Bay'.

Most weekday evenings, we would head down to one of the two youth clubs in Benwell; the Moorside or the Avellan. My favourite was the Avellan, on the corner of Armstrong Road and Condingham Road. Before entering, we would pass around the customary bottle of Strongbow cider, knowing that once inside we would be fuelled by nothing but copious amounts of Coca-Cola. We would hang around by the 'flipper machine' and occasionally venture into the disco room next door. When the right tune came on we would swagger onto the dance floor and try our best to look cool and hard.

I was also getting into Tamla Motown and, whereas when we danced to Ska or Reggae we would stand in a circle and dance on our own, the sweet sounds of Marvin Gaye and Diana Ross provided the perfect opportunity to dance with a 'bird'. It was thanks to Motown that I met my first serious girlfriend.

Rosie Farrow in Levi's jeans, oxblood riding boots, a Fred Perry t-shirt and a Harrington jacket was a vision that was hard to resist. As *I Heard It Through the Grapevine* crackled through the disco, I crossed the dance floor. No words were spoken between us. I just gave her a nod that meant 'fancy a dance?' She nodded back. I was in.

Pretty soon, we were 'babysitting' at Rosie's house, even though there were no babies to sit. This was just an excuse to have the place to ourselves while her parents were out for the evening. Rosie had a sister called Liz and me and my mate Keith would do what would now be called 'double-dating'. After a couple of cans of cider, we would split off into pairs and head to the bedrooms. Whatever we got up to, we had to make sure that it was over by the time the girls' parents came back. Not that we got up to much; an 'inside top' was the best that could be expected. But you've got to start somewhere.

On Saturday evenings, I would often babysit our Tony and Suzanne; the perfect excuse to get the girls around. I just had to be sure that they had left before my mam and dad got back, just before eleven. By that time, I would have tidied up the house and I would be in the middle of watching *Match of the Day*. As soon as they came through the door, my dad would send me off to bed. I found it strange that I was considered old enough to be left with my younger brother and sister but not to stay up beyond eleven. I had devised a plan, though: I would leave the living room door open and sit on the stairs so that I could watch the games through the door.

Though my mam and dad would return in a good mood, often it would be broken when my dad, from out of nowhere, would accuse my mam of looking at some bloke. My mam would reply that she didn't know what he was talking about and she hadn't been looking at anyone. He would accuse her of stuff that she wasn't guilty of and then she would start accusing him of things that he *was* guilty of. He would regularly succumb to the old cliché of coming home with 'lipstick on his collar'.

Their rows became more frequent and would no longer be confined to a Saturday night. My dad was still working away and often things would 'kick off' when my mam saw him packing his bag. She would ask him why he needed to pack a suit when he was working in the middle of the North Sea. He said he needed it for work. Once, she held up a pair of ski boots that he was packing, along with what looked suspiciously like a pair of snow goggles. He tried in vain to convince my mam that these were his work boots and welding goggles. He must have been the only bloke on the rig that welded in a suit, ski boots and snow goggles.

What became evident was that he wasn't coming home after he had finished his stint offshore; he was spending weekends with his mates in Aberdeen or even on the ski slopes of Aviemore. Whatever he was up to, for the time being my mam seemed happy to turn a blind eye.

HAIRY MUSIC

STAIRWAY TO HEAVEN

One night, I was heading into town on the 33 bus when I spotted a bunch of lads from school hanging around the bus stop on Adelaide Terrace. One of them was Paul Reeve, who I had spoken to in the school yard a couple of days earlier; I had asked him why he had 'Starman' written in blue ink on the back of his hand. Paul had explained that the previous night he had seen David Bowie perform that song on *Top of the Pops*. The note was to remind him to ask his mam, who worked in the record department of Windows music shop in the centre of Newcastle, to get the record for him.

Paul saw me sitting at the back of the bus and waved me down. He introduced me to his mates: Les Sunderland, Keith Lowes, Robin Ridley and Mick Thomson, telling them, "This is Bob, he's really into music." One of them asked me what I was into, and what was the last record that I had bought. As it happened, I had just bought my first-ever single, Gary Glitter's *I Didn't Know I Loved You Till I Saw You Rock and Roll*. At the time I thought that Gary Glitter was fantastic and to me he was up there alongside Elvis Presley. Aside from listening to Ska and Motown back in 1972, Gary was my main man. In fact, many years later I even grew a bit of a Gary Glitter haircut; not that this is something I would ever admit to now. When I told the lads of my most recent purchase they started pissing themselves laughing but they didn't seem to hold it against me. They went on to ask, "What was the last album you bought?" Well, at the time I didn't own any albums but, rather than admit this, I told them I wasn't into albums and that I preferred singles.

Eventually, the conversation turned to *Monty Python*, a popular television series at the time. I had watched a couple of episodes but didn't really like it. I enjoyed the animation but didn't really get the sketches. It turned out that these blokes could recite whole chunks of the dialogue. I could tell you who played centre-half for Newcastle United, and what was the best colour Sta Prest, but as far as reciting the 'dead parrot sketch', I didn't have a clue. Just as I was about to say I had to be somewhere, Paul suggested we go back to his.

I wasn't sure about going along as I felt a bit out of my depth but thank god I did. I wasn't to know it at the time but it was one of the best decisions I ever made.

Paul Reeve lived on the third floor of a block of flats called Adelaide House. His mam was really friendly and asked us if we would like a cup of tea or something to eat. Loaded up with tea and sandwiches, we went into Paul's room. So this was what it was like to have your own space, and not have to share with your brother. The room was lit by a single red bulb and the walls were covered with posters: Led Zeppelin, the Who and Jimi Hendrix. Paul also had his own record player and a massive collection of albums. I was still using my dad's gramophone to play my record collection, which consisted of one single.

We found a place to sit, on the floor or on the bed, as Paul put on the latest album by Led Zeppelin. I wouldn't have known who it was, it didn't even have the name of the group on the cover; just a photo of an old tramp carrying a load of sticks on his back. No one spoke, we just nodded in approval as the music blasted out of the record player. Any minute now I was expecting Paul's mam to come in and tell us to turn it down and, sure enough, she did pop her head around the door but, rather than tell us to 'turn that racket down', she asked if any of us would like another cup of tea.

We must have sat there listening to music for around five hours. Zeppelin were followed onto the turntable by albums by Deep Purple, Black Sabbath, Wishbone Ash, Free, the Who, Hawkwind, and a Jimi Hendrix album called *Wow*, which I learned was not an 'official album' but a bootleg recording of his live performances. Aside from the Who and Free, whose singles I had heard on the radio, this was a whole new world for me. Ska was great for dancing to. Motown had great tunes, and lyrics about broken hearts. This was something else. I have never been able to put into words what it was about this music that caused it to have such an effect on me but there was something about those guitars, drums and voices that seemed to arrive at just the right time in my life and, from that moment on, things would never be the same.

Within the space of a couple of months, my short hair had grown over my shoulders and my Harrington jacket had been replaced by a Levi denim jacket. My skinhead days were over but my years as a hairy had just begun.

TAKE IT EASY

One of our mates, Robin Ridley, had two older brothers; Carl and Martin. They were into 'West Coast' music and pretty soon we were listening to albums by the likes of the Eagles and Jackson Browne, alongside Sabbath and Zeppelin. The Eagles offered a very different experience to British bands. Zeppelin's Robert Plant was singing about how he was being mistreated by some baby or other, and of ladies who were buying a Stairway to Heaven. Ozzy Osbourne from Sabbath was singing about drugs and death. The Eagles, however, were singing about highways and deserts and Winslow, Arizona; places where you could drink Tequila and watch the sunrise, while hanging out with 'Witchy Women'. As a fifteen-year-old drinking bottles of cider on the Pipe Track Lane, they fired my imagination and got me thinking that maybe one day I might get to visit these mystical places that existed only on records, films and TV.

This was an education unlike the one that I was getting at school and it would hold me in good stead in the years that lay ahead. I learned the names of the band members; which guitars they played; the amplifiers they used; where their albums were recorded; who designed the album sleeves; who produced and engineered the albums. You very rarely saw any of these groups on the telly so you would learn what they looked like and what they had to say by poring over the *New Musical Express*, *Melody Maker* and *Sounds*.

Sounds was always a personal favourite of mine as it came with a free poster and soon my bedroom wall was covered. One poster that found a space on my wall featured Dave Cousins from the Strawbs. I hadn't even heard any of their records but he looked the part. When I did hear their music, he came down off the wall and was replaced by a poster of Eric Clapton wearing a white suit and playing a black-and-white Fender Stratocaster. He looked like the coolest thing on the planet.

For Christmas 1972, I got a record player of my own and, along with it, my first-ever album, *Black Sabbath Volume Four*. I must have played that album a hundred times a day; it was the most brilliant thing that I had ever heard. I even painted my haversack that I carried my school books in with a copy of the silhouette of Ozzy which graced the cover of the album. The inside cover had a shot of the band taken from the back of the stage so that you could see the crowd in front of them. I would imagine what it must have been like to be part of that crowd, to not only hear the music but to see it performed. As yet I had not been to a live concert.

Every month there seemed to be a new album that you had to listen to. I remember the feeling of excitement among my friends when we heard that a new release by Pink Floyd was imminent. I must be honest and admit that I was never really a massive fan of Floyd. For me, they never delivered the bombast and the excitement of Zeppelin or the Who, or the blues undertones of Free or the Stones. I always felt that I was missing something. Maybe this new album would be the one when I got 'the Floyd'. All the reviews were telling us that this forthcoming album, *Dark Side of the Moon*, was their masterpiece.

We all sat around in Paul's bedroom in preparation for the first-ever playback of the album. We drew the curtains and sat in almost complete darkness, aside from the solitary red light bulb. We had even bought a bunch of joss sticks which we thought would add to the vibe. The needle was dropped on side one. We waited for the magic to fill the room. We got to the end of the first side and no one had spoken a word. Paul turned the record over and played the second side. At the end he said, "Well, what do you think?"

We all agreed it certainly sounded different; in fact, it sounded quite scary. But we came to the conclusion that whatever it was that the reviewers had heard, somehow it wasn't connecting with us. We realised that we were missing an essential ingredient that would no doubt unleash the greatness concealed within the grooves of the album.

DRUGS

These days, if you believe what you read in the press, getting hold of drugs is as easy as it looks in an episode of *The Wire*, with a drug dealer on every street corner offering you a smorgasbord of delights. Well, I can tell you that was certainly not the case in Newcastle in the early 1970s. You would have more chance of getting hold of a lump of kryptonite than a lump of hash. LSD was something that only existed in San Francisco, cocaine just a name that Geezer Butler from Black Sabbath was telling us to enjoy via a logo on his t-shirt. But rumour was that you could 'score some pot' at the Old George; a 'hairy pub' situated just off the Bigg Market in Newcastle. Whether or not this was true, we were never going to be able to find out. The chances of the doorman letting a bunch of sixteen-year-olds climb the stairs to the upstairs bar, to ask the barman if he knew where we could get hold of 'something a little stronger' were slim. But we were desperate, we wanted drugs, and we wanted them now.

It was decided that the only place to score was London. For a couple of quid, you could jump on the National Express bus, which six hours later would drop you in the 'drug capital' of the UK. We had no doubt that scoring in London would be as easy as getting off the bus at Victoria, heading over to Soho, and asking the first long-haired person you met, "Have you got any drugs?"

What could be easier?

The hard part was deciding who was going to volunteer to be our drug runner. Before we got around to drawing straws, Steve Baker spoke up. "I fancy a day trip to London, I'll do it." Steve explained to us that he had been to London before and this would give him an advantage over any of us as he pretty much knew his way around. Steve later told us that his parents had taken him on a trip to London when he was ten years old.

On the day of the trip, Steve left Newcastle early on the London bus and we waited excitedly for his return. The following day, he was back with his tail between his legs. He told us there weren't any drugs to be had in London. We thought that maybe he had 'done them all in' himself. But a couple of days later, he admitted that he had in fact 'scored'. As Steve explained, when he had come out of the tube at Piccadilly, he was approached by a bloke who asked him if he was looking to score. This was easier than he could ever have imagined. The guy had told Steve to follow him and, in a back lane off Shaftesbury avenue, Steve handed over his money and the guy slipped him half an ounce of black, telling him to go easy on it as it was 'really strong'. Before boarding the bus back to Newcastle, Steve thought he had better 'knock one up' to see how good the gear really was; no doubt thinking it would help take the edge off the coach journey. On unwrapping the silver paper, he broke a bit off the edge of his block and rolled himself a fat one. As he was just about to take his first 'toke', he noticed that his fingers were black. Upon closer inspection, he realised that he had rolled a joint from a block of black shoe polish. It looked like his days as a drug mule were going to end as quickly as they had begun.

Steve was able to redeem himself when, just a few weeks later, he arrived at Paul's with a bag of hemp seeds. Whether or not this qualified as drugs, we were not sure, but we were all excited to give it a go. We rolled a joint and, before lighting it, began discussing what would be the best album to enhance our first drug experience. Hendrix or the Floyd would have been the obvious choice but I had other ideas as to what music would best serve to accompany us on our virgin voyage into the unknown. I had recently purchased *The Faust Tapes* by the German group Faust.

One of the reasons I had bought it was because it had a great sleeve. But the main reason was because it sold for forty-nine pence, the price of a single. However, as I had quickly discovered, not only did the group sing in German but none of the tracks on the album had any names. The record's label simply said 'Side One' and 'Side Two' so I couldn't even tell you which were the stand-out tracks. This album would be the perfect litmus test as to how good the drugs were. If the drugs could make the Faust album sound even half-decent, we were onto a winner.

We passed the joint around and took a couple of big hits each. I began to feel a bit light-headed and then like I was going to throw up. I am not sure whether this was the effect of the drugs or the music, or a mixture of both. If the album had suddenly started sounding great I am certain that I would have ended up a fully-fledged pothead but as it happened it still sounded like shite.

DO YOU REMEMBER THE SATURDAY GIGS?

As the summer of 1972 was coming to an end, I still had yet to witness any of the bands that I loved playing live in concert. Before I could tick that box, I had to start earning some money. A couple of my mates had got part-time jobs at the Scotswood Social Club, as floor waiters. They mentioned that there was a job coming up as one of them had been promoted to barman. I went along for an interview and I got the job.

Being a floor waiter meant you were given a float of twenty pounds and would take drinks orders off the customers at their table then go to the bar and pay for the drinks with the money from your float. My mate working behind the bar would give us the drinks without charging us. When we took the drinks to the table, the money for them would go down our socks. Many nights we would limp out of the club with a sock full of loose change. Thanks to my proceeds from 'working' at the club, on 15th December 1972 I got to see my first-ever live concert.

A couple of months earlier, we had read in *Sounds* that Hawkwind were planning a tour and would be playing Newcastle City Hall. Hawkwind were not my favourite band but it had also been announced that as part of this tour the band would be augmented by the addition of a new member called Stacia who during the concert would do an interpretive dance to the music, semi-naked. This was almost too good to be true: my first chance to see a live band and, thrown into the bargain, get to look at a pair of breasts.

The morning that the tickets were on sale, I got the bus with Paul

Reeve and Mick Thomson to get to the City Hall really early. We joined the queue behind a hundred fellow 'Hawkwind Freaks'. At ten o'clock the doors were opened and fifteen minutes later we were being shown a seating plan by the lady in the box office. We chose the seats as close to the front of the stage as possible; we had been hoping for front row but had to settle for the centre of row D. We handed over £1.60, for two tickets each. We took our tickets home, duly pinned them to our bedroom walls, and counted down the weeks until the night of the gig.

When the time came, we gathered in the City Tavern pub, just along the road from the venue, and had a couple of pints to get us in the mood. Mick Thomson had already seen Led Zeppelin, who had played the City Hall a month earlier. Zeppelin had now replaced Sabbath as my favourite band; I still loved Sabbath but Zeppelin took it to a whole other level. I would have killed to have seen Zeppelin, but Hawkwind were a good place to start.

We got to our seats early to soak up the pre-gig atmosphere. I stood and looked around the City Hall; it seemed massive but in fact only held a couple of thousand people. We stood there checking out the gear that the band were using, the amps and the drum kit. Before the start of the gig, an announcement was made over the PA that Stacia would not be appearing. Our collective hearts sank but all was not lost as we were then informed that there would be a replacement dancer.

At what must have been around 9pm, the lights were dimmed and a giant cheer went up. When the band came on stage and kicked into *Technicians of Space Ship Earth* from the recently released *In Search of Space* album, the crowd around us went crazy. I had never heard anything so loud in all my life; I had listened to these songs on the album but this took it to a whole new level. I couldn't make out what instruments were playing; it was just a wall of sound, but it was so fucking exciting. I looked to my left, where Mick Thomson was standing. He was already 'getting into it'; his eyes were tightly shut and he was playing an invisible guitar then would switch to invisible drums, all the while shaking his head in time to the music. This now would be called headbanging but back in '72 the phrase had not even been invented. Mick was 'freaking out' and I thought, if you can't beat 'em, join 'em. I still had one eye on the stage as I didn't want to miss anything. Not that I could make out any of the band members as the stage was covered in dry ice but, sure enough, there in amongst the band was the unmistakable form of a scantily clad woman. Imagine my disappointment when the dry ice finally cleared and Stacia's replacement turned out to be a much larger lady. Even more disappointing, she decided to keep her top on. We all felt a bit cheated but it was still a great gig. One down, thousands to go.

During the next few months, we would repeat the ritual of getting down to the City Hall really early on the day tickets went on sale, to try and get the best seats possible. We saw some fantastic gigs: Deep Purple, Wishbone Ash and Uriah Heep. But it's not just the great gigs that stick in your mind; some were just as memorable for all the wrong reasons. We had read a fantastic review of *Birds of Fire*, the new album by the Mahavishnu Orchestra; by all accounts the group's guitarist John McLaughlin was one of the greatest guitarists in the world. When we turned up at the box office, we were delighted to discover that we were first in line and were able to get front row seats.

John walked on stage wearing a white suit and carrying a double-neck Gibson guitar. This looked very promising. I was a bit surprised when he bowed to the audience as if in prayer, then sat on a stool at the front of the stage. Then the band started playing. It seemed like they were all playing a different tune, or maybe they were still tuning up; whatever they were doing, it didn't sound like a song. It lasted about twenty minutes and there was no singing. I also noticed that none of the audience were 'freaking out'; just sitting nodding in appreciation.

At one point, someone in the audience walked to the front of the stage and took a photograph of John McLaughlin. As the flash went off, John opened his eyes and gave the guy a withering look, shook his head, and mouthed the words 'no photographs'. Because we were in the front row, we were scared to get up and leave, for fear that we too would suffer the wrath of John. We sat there for what seemed like hours, as one drawn-out dirge followed another. I am sure they were great musicians but they seemed to be playing for themselves. I later learned that this was what was termed 'jazz rock'. It was the first and last jazz rock gig that I ever attended.

The Odeon Cinema would also host gigs when the City Hall was not available, or maybe because the Odeon had a larger capacity. I never enjoyed the Odeon gigs as much as those at the City Hall as it just felt like a cinema masquerading as a music venue, so there was a slight feeling of disappointment when it was announced that the Who would be playing the Odeon on their upcoming tour.

Of all the bands that I had seen to date, the Who were the band that I was most excited at the prospect of seeing. Pete Townshend was my favourite songwriter and Roger Daltrey was up there alongside Robert Plant as one of my favourite singers. When Roger sang about a 'teenage wasteland' during *Baba O'Riley* or how we would be 'fighting in the street' on *Won't Get Fooled Again,* I felt as though he was singing about me and my mates. Townshend might have been writing about Shepherd's Bush in London but it could just as easily have been Benwell in Newcastle.

To be sure of getting tickets for the gig, we decided that we would camp overnight outside the Queen's Cinema, where the tickets were going to be on sale. We arrived early evening, armed with our sleeping bags, sandwiches and cans of beer, and took our place on the steps outside. We were the first in line. Pretty soon, more fans started arriving and the line stretched around the block. When the pubs started kicking out at ten-thirty, a few fights broke out when some blokes thought they would jump the queue. The thing about the Who fans was that they were harder than your average peace-loving rock music fan and any potential queue-jumpers were soon sent packing.

Throughout the night, we kept our spirits up by singing Who songs and two hours before the box office opened we climbed out of our sleeping bags and waited for the doors to be unlocked. Our sleepless night was worthwhile. We were rewarded with front row seats.

When the night of the gig arrived three months later, we took our seats to discover that there was an orchestra pit in front of the stage. Even though we were in the front row, there was still a big space between us and the band. When they came on, we rushed to the front of the orchestra pit but were pushed back into our seats by the bouncers. This was no way to watch the Who.

A month prior to the gig, the band had released their double *Quadrophenia* album and aside from the single *5.15* we had yet to familiarise ourselves with the songs. We were hoping that they would play more of their classics but it seemed they were going to be playing mainly songs from the new album. *Quadrophenia* was another of Pete Townshend's concept albums and, despite reading the album sleeve notes, we were not sure what the concept was. The band were using backing tapes during the gig but they didn't seem to be working and Townshend seemed in a really bad mood. He did smash up his guitar, which was great, but overall the show was not what we had hoped.

Afterwards, despite a feeling of disappointment, we decided to go around to the stage door in the hope that we might meet the band. Just as we were about to give up, the door opened and out walked Pete Townshend, followed by Roger Daltrey. The first thing I noticed was how small Daltrey was; he had looked ten-foot-tall when we had seen him on stage. Townshend, on the other hand, must have been over six foot, and he had a massive nose. I passed Townshend a piece of paper and in my excitement said, "Keith, can you sign this?" Townshend replied, "Keith? I'm not bloody Keith, he's the drummer." I was devastated. I felt like I had made a fool of myself, not only in front of my mates but also in front of Pete Townshend and Roger Daltrey. However, Pete gave us the plastic cup that he was drinking out of and in the bottom was a half-inch of brandy. We passed it around.

Meeting the band had made up for the disappointment of the gig. The next day, we were telling our mates that we had met Pete and Roger after the gig and had a drink with them. There was no mention of my faux pas.

INTO THE VALLEY

The Who would have the chance to redeem themselves after the disappointment of the Odeon concert. They announced that they would be playing a one-day festival at Charlton Athletic football ground in London. For me this would be a double first: the first time that I had been to London, and my first music festival.

On the evening of Friday 17ᵗʰ May 1974, me and my mates Paul Reeve, Steve Baker, Mick Thomson, John Hardy and Graham Balantyne boarded the overnight bus from Gallowgate coach station for what was going to be a six-hour bus journey to London. Prior to heading into town to catch the coach, we had met at Paul's mam's and loaded up with enough beer to open a brewery. By the time we took our seats at the back of the bus, we had already lightened our load. It seemed that everyone on the bus was going to the gig and the party was starting early. As we pulled out of the bus station, a cheer went up and we burst into the popular ditty that accompanied many a school bus trip: 'Oh the driver's got the wind up.'

Half an hour later, we were approaching Durham and by then we were well into a rousing version of the Who's *Magic Bus*, a song we thought fitting to our situation. We had just ended the line thanking the driver 'for getting us here' when the bus lurched to a stop. Great, I thought, this must be the first of what I hoped would be many toilet stops. But, before any of us could get up, the driver stormed to the back of the bus, pointed at the six of us and said, "You lot, off my bus, if you think that I'm putting up with that racket for six hours you've got another thing coming." Of all the people who were sitting on the bus, he had singled out the six of us. There were many others who were as vocal as we were but for some reason we were the ones who were about to be sacrificed. We pleaded with the driver, who was obviously not a Who fan, and promised that we would stop singing, but he was not having any of it.

Before we knew it, we were stood on the pavement as the coach pulled away. We were stranded in Durham, close to tears. The only thing to do was walk to Durham Station and catch a train back to Newcastle. When we got to the station, we noticed that there was a train due in fifteen minutes that was heading to London. To catch the train would cost us most of our spending money. But it was either that or miss the gig.

So it was that we arrived by train into King's Cross at six o'clock in the morning, relieved of most of our spending money and all of what we had thought was our endless supply of booze. Through bleary eyes and with raging hangovers, we had our first glimpse of London. What a shithole. On the journey across the city to Charlton, we sat and stared out of the train window.

"Bloody hell, who would want to live here?" one of the lads commented and we all nodded in agreement. We passed through a landscape of disused factories and what looked like slum houses that backed onto the railway lines. It looked like most of the people who lived in the houses hadn't bothered with curtains and had just slung bed sheets across the windows. Even though the train was full, none of the other passengers seemed very happy; they just sat in silence. And this was a Saturday - I would have hated to see how miserable they looked on a Monday morning.

From Charlton train station, we followed the crowd who were heading towards 'The Valley'; home of Charlton Athletic FC. The ground seemed to be in the middle of a housing estate and looked the most unlikely place to hold a music festival. Feeling a little bit tired and deflated, and so far not too impressed by our first day in the big city, we stood and waited for the gates to open. We were starving and chipped in what we had left of our money, to buy a load of pies and some beers to keep us going through the day. We were shocked to discover that what we had was only enough to buy twenty beers and one pie each. Bloody hell, how did people afford to eat in London? In Newcastle we could have bought a bakery for what we had just paid for six pies.

At around eleven o'clock, the gates opened and we found a good spot in the middle of the pitch. We seemed to be the only people around who were not smoking weed but the sun was shining and that was enough to get us in the mood. Our spirits were raised even further as soon as the music started. First on the bill were Montrose; none of us had heard of them before but they sounded enough like Led Zeppelin to win our approval and their lead singer, Sammy Hager, looked like a dead ringer for Robert Plant. Bad Company, the new band that had been formed by Paul Rodgers after Free had broken up, came on next. I had seen Bad Company do a sound check at Newcastle City Hall a couple of months earlier for what was to be their debut gig, but had to leave early to go to my job at the working men's club. It was a bonus to finally get to see them.

Next up were our local boys, Lindisfarne. I had never been a big fan of theirs as they always sounded a bit folky for my liking but we had to support our local lads, raising our voices and singing along to *Fog on the Tyne* and *Meet Me on the Corner*. I missed most of Stone the Crows as I had gone to find a toilet. By the time I got back and found my mates, the band had already finished their set and were making way for Lou Reed.

Dressed in black leather, with his hair dyed bright orange, Lou came mincing onto the stage as the band cranked out *Sweet Jane*. One of the first things Lou did, even before he had reached the microphone to sing the first line of the song, was throw his drink into the crowd, a large section of which responded by throwing their drinks back. Having made the journey to find the toilet, my bet was that those nearest the front of the stage had not been bothered to do the same and had instead relieved themselves into the receptacles that were now scattered around Lou's feet and whose contents were running down his leather strides. Lou seemed to be in a bit of a bad mood and didn't really look like he had entered into the spirit of things. He was probably wishing that he was hanging out with Andy Warhol in New York rather than appearing in front of all these hippies at a 'soccer' stadium in East London.

Humble Pie were the last act on before the headliners. Their singer Steve Marriott had previously been in the Small Faces and I had pretty much written them off as being a pop band, even though I had loved the song *All or Nothing*. Steve Marriot was a singer that I had overlooked but on this day he was fantastic. The guitar that he was playing, a black Les Paul, was almost as big as he was and I made a mental note to check out some of their records when I got back home.

But the highlight of the day was the Who. They were everything they had not been six months earlier when I had seen them at the Odeon. They kicked off with *Can't Explain* and didn't let up for two hours. They played a selection of songs from *Quadrophenia*, but mixed them in with *Won't Get Fooled Again* and *Baba O'Riley*. At one point, Townshend mentioned that the last time he had seen a crowd like this was when the Who had performed at Woodstock. This quote resonated with me and my mates as this was our Woodstock.

We caught the last train out of Charlton and made our way to Victoria Coach Station. We felt like soldiers returning from the front. We were tired and hungry; so tired, in fact, that as we waited in the crowded bus station, Mick Thomson proved the theory that you can fall asleep standing up. Luckily for us, the driver on the return leg was not the same guy who had cut short our outward journey.

It was another milestone to tick off; we had attended our first music festival. We dragged our weary bodies to the back of the bus and sat in silence as we pulled out of Victoria and started our long journey home through the night.

IF YOU WANNA BE A SINGER OR PLAY GUITAR

Music was now pretty much taking over my life and my mates were the same. It was all about music: watching it being performed; listening to it; reading about it; talking about it. The next stage was to have a go at playing it. We all agreed that the only instrument any of us were interested in was the guitar. None of us had any desire to play the bass, only someone who was mad would be interested in playing the drums, and who would want to be sat behind a keyboard? But before we got to the point of playing a guitar, just to hold one in our hands would be a giant leap forward. The problem was that up to this point in our lives we had only ever seen Gibson Les Pauls or Fender Stratocasters in the hands of the guitarists that we worshipped. Jimmy Page, Eric Clapton, Pete Townshend, Paul Kossoff and Jimi Hendrix lived nowhere near Benwell so it was unlikely they would be 'giving us a go' on their guitars. However, there was one person who did live in Benwell and who, as legend would have it, was the owner of a Fender Strat. That was Stewart Selkirk.

Robin Ridley had once roadied for the band that Stew played in and knew that he lived just up the road from Paul Reeve's house, in Colston Street. Four of us walked up the hill from Paul's and knocked on Stew's door. It was opened by a really handsome bloke, a couple of years older than us, who had really long hair. He looked like a rock star. I knew it must be Stew.

I was pushed to the front of the queue. "Hello Stew, I'm Bob and these are my mates, Paul and Mick. Robin told us that you have a

Fender Strat, is there any chance we might have a look at it, please?"

Whatever he thought of a bunch of young kids turning up at his front door, asking to see his guitar, I never found out, but Stew gave us a knowing smile and in a friendly voice replied, "Yeah, sure guys, come on up."

We followed him up the stairs that led to his flat and there on the chair in front of us was the most beautiful thing that we had ever set eyes upon. Sue Nelson. The best looking girl in Benwell. We had all heard of her and I am sure that I once passed her in the street, but up this close she looked even better.

"Sue, meet Bob, Robin, Mick and Paul; they've come to see my Strat." Sue just smiled at us as if four guys turning up in her boyfriend's front room to look at his guitar was an everyday occurrence. Stew pulled a guitar case out from behind the sofa and opened it. Lying on a bed of red velvet was his Strat. Like Sue, it was also blonde and a thing of true beauty.

Stew lifted the guitar from his case, sat down on his sofa and played a few runs on the guitar. It wasn't plugged into an amp but it still sounded great.

"Would any of you like a play?" Robin stepped forward and took the guitar from Stew, nodded and said, "Yeah, great action." The guitar was then passed to Mick before it eventually came to me. As I held it, something seemed wrong. It felt uncomfortable in my hands. Stew laughed and said, "Hey Bob, you're a left-hander." Shit, this was a disaster. I felt comforted when Stew pointed out to me that Hendrix was also a left-hander and how that had not been a hindrance to him becoming the greatest guitar player that ever lived.

We sat and chatted with Stew for a while then thanked him for showing us his Strat and, with one more look at Sue, walked out of Stew's house. We'd never been interested in playing anything but the guitar and now, having had the chance to hold a Strat ourselves, that idea was firmly cemented. I doubt that Stew would have been sitting up there in his flat with Sue Nelson if it had been a drum kit stashed behind his sofa. We had been to 'the mountain' and we had heard the word, and the word was 'guitars'.

The Saturday following our exodus to visit Stew's Strat, the four of us paid a visit to Jeavons music store, on New Bridge Street in Newcastle. Jeavons had been featured in the Bob Dylan movie *Don't Look Back*; Bob is filmed looking at guitars in the shop window. What was good enough for Bob was good enough for us. Not that I would have professed to being into Dylan at the time as, like Lindisfarne, as far as I was concerned, Dylan fell into the category of 'folky'. It was only many years later that the scales fell from my eyes as to Bob's genius.

We all knew that Jimmy Page played a Les Paul and that Hendrix played a Strat; you were either a Fender or Gibson man, and those were the two makes of guitar that we all wanted. Unfortunately, there was a shortage of Gibsons and Fenders in the shop and those that were there were well out of our price range. But, as the salesman pointed out, there was a plentiful supply of what we were told were really good copies by Antoria, Selmer and CSL. They looked pretty much the same as the real thing but sold for less than half the price. We returned from Jeavons laden with guitar brochures.

Years later, I met Mark Knopfler from Dire Straits and he told me how, when he was a kid, he too would collect guitar brochures, and would actually smell the pages. We never went quite this far but we did spend endless hours looking at 'guitar porn', discussing the guitar that each of us would buy once we had saved up enough money. For me, money was going to be the problem; I no longer had my floor waiter job as the club secretary had eventually noticed that they were selling more beer than the takings at the till would attest. Before the finger of suspicion was pointed at me, I quit. As things stood, there was no way that I was going to be able to afford even a copy guitar, at least not until I left school and found a job, and that was still a year away.

I'M A ROAD RUNNER, BABY!

Over the following months, Keith Lowes, Paul Reeve and Robin Ridley all bought guitars. Talk turned to the idea that we should form a band. We would gather in Paul's bedroom and I would sit and watch as they worked out simple guitar riffs. The frustrating thing was that, being left-handed, I couldn't even have a go on their guitars; the strings were upside-down. By the time I would be able to afford a guitar, they would be streets ahead of me and, even if I turned out to be a fast learner, even Lynyrd Skynyrd only had three lead guitarists. Four would be stretching it a bit.

Stew Selkirk told us that he was putting a new band together and asked if any of us would like to come and watch them rehearse. Paul and I thought that was a good idea. We were picked up from Stew's in the band's transit van. Just to be sat in the back with the gear and the rest of the guys was great; this was the life that we aspired to. When we reached Blucher Working Men's club, in Throckley on the outskirts of Newcastle, Paul and I helped the guys load out their gear. I thought that maybe if I impressed Stew, he might give me a job as a roadie for his new band. Once they had set up, Paul and I sat and listened as they ran through their material. Alongside songs by the Beatles and the Stones, they were also rehearsing *The Jean Genie* by David Bowie. Stew said that he couldn't remember all the words. When I said I knew them, Stew suggested I sing. OK, I thought, I'll give it a go. I grabbed hold of the mic and stood stock-still as the band played the intro. This was the first time I had ever sung into a microphone. I heard my voice coming through the PA system and, with a bit of reverb on, I thought I sounded half-decent.

By the time we had reached the last verse, I felt confident enough to open my eyes. I looked into the empty concert room and could see Paul, who smiled and gave me a thumbs-up. The song seemed to only last seconds; before I knew it, it was over. Stew shook my hand and told me, "Hey Bob, you've got a really strong voice." Coming from Stew, this comment was high praise indeed. I jumped down and walked back to where Paul was sitting. My legs were shaking and, despite only being up on that stage for less than four minutes, I could feel sweat running down my back. It was almost like having sex for the first time; I was a bit scared but I really enjoyed it and couldn't wait to do it again.

As we were packing away the band's gear, Paul suggested that, rather than buy a guitar, I buy a microphone and become the singer in our band. This was just about within my price range and it also meant that I didn't need to buy an amp. Before we got back to Benwell, it was settled. I was the singer.

Paul decided that our nascent band needed a name. Originally, we were going to be Frendz but that name only lasted one night. Then it was going to be Geordie, until we discovered that another local band had beaten us to it. Eventually, we called ourselves Road Runner, after the cartoon character that appeared on the telly. We also thought it had a bluesy sound to it.

We had a band and, now the band had a name, everyone wanted to be part of it.

Ges Sydenham bought a keyboard and Tony Willi bought a bass guitar. All we needed was a drummer. Paul's cousin Steve Baker, our failed drug runner, put himself forward. Despite not owning a drum kit, Steve had the ability to make us laugh at the drop of a hat, and had a slight air of madness about him; attributes that we felt were needed to be a drummer. What also worked in his favour was that he shared the same surname as Ginger, the drummer from Cream. When he eventually bought himself a drum kit, he was a natural, as we expected.

Not only could he hold down a good beat, he totally looked the part.

Up to this point, Paul Reeve's mam had been happy to let us rehearse in his bedroom but one night, after an extended version of Led Zeppelin's *Moby Dick*, she popped her head around the door and suggested that we might start to look for a new place to rehearse. We ended up at a scout hut in Silver Lonnen, having convinced the guy who ran the place that we were a folk group. He must have been surprised when we turned up for our first rehearsal and he saw the amount of gear we had. I imagine he must have thought we were a folk group who, like Dylan had done, were just about to 'go electric'.

Pretty soon, we had learnt around a dozen songs. *Smoke on the Water* by Deep Purple, *The Hunter* by Free, *Hi Ho Silver Lining* by Jeff Beck, *Sunshine of Your Love* by Cream and *Paranoid* by Sabbath. I am sure that at the time there must have been a thousand bands all over the UK learning the same set of songs, but Road Runner had an ace up our sleeve. I might not have been the greatest singer in Benwell but I was the only one, as far as I knew, who could by vocal prowess alone replicate the synthesizer line from Hawkwind's *Silver Machine*. When I first performed this feat of vocal wonderment, the rest of the band were gobsmacked. Who needed a synth player in the band when they had me?

Steve Reay, a friend of ours, would watch us rehearse and tell us how great we sounded. One night, he turned up with another guy in tow. While we were packing away our gear, Steve introduced his friend, Derek, as the manager of a band called Wild Honey, who were doing the rounds in Throckley. Steve explained that Wild Honey's lead singer was going on holiday at the same time that they were due to perform at a local youth club and that Derek had been impressed by me and wondered if I fancied filling in for the gig. Derek said that, aside from *Silver Machine*, Wild Honey were pretty much playing the same group of songs as we were and that after a couple of rehearsals I would be ready for the gig.

Three weeks later, I was backstage at Throckley Youth Centre. This would be my debut performance in front of a live audience. The last time I had sung in front of a crowd was back at South Benwell Junior School when I was around ten years old. I was petrified. Steve Reay did nothing to settle my pre-gig nerves when he pointed out that this was no longer a rehearsal, this was the real thing and, as the front man in the band, I had to look the part. Steve produced a pair of jeans that were a dead ringer for those worn by Paul Rodgers during his days in Free. Rodgers had accessorised his Levi's by putting silver metal studs down both the outside and inside seams. At the bottom, the studs would follow the line of the flare as they covered his desert boots. Steve suggested this was the look I needed. I tried them on and they looked great.

We had decided that we would kick off our set with Free's *Alright Now*. The version we were doing was the one that had appeared on the album *Free Live*. This kicks off with a drum intro, which we had decided to extend before the guitars kicked in. The plan was that halfway through this extended introduction I would come strutting onto the stage. Or at least I would have come strutting onto the stage had I not had what must have been around ten pounds of metal down the sides of my jeans. I could hardly walk, never mind strut.

By the time we were into our second song, *Paranoid*, my pained expression had little to do with singing about my state of mind and more with my imagining the state of my legs where the studs were digging into my skin. Paul Rodgers' mam must have stitched material into the seams inside his jeans to prevent her son's legs being lacerated; something that Steve's mam had not considered.

I managed to make it through our forty-five-minute set and dragged myself, limping, back to our dressing room. When I peeled off my jeans, which were attached to my skin in a hundred places, it looked like I had been attacked by a crocodile. However, aside from the wounds on my legs, which would take weeks to heal, I had made it through my first-ever gig relatively unscathed and Derek told me he thought that I had done a great job. Although I was a bit disappointed that I had not been offered the job full-time, I was soon back with Road Runner and hungry to do more gigs. However, after six months of rehearsals, we still hadn't got around to playing to an audience. It soon became clear that these particular Road Runners didn't have the legs to go the distance.

We had all harboured dreams of making it as musicians but, as the summer of 1974 approached, I could see that interest in the band was starting to wane and that the reality of going out into the big world was looming. We were approaching the end of our final school year and those of us not staying on at school had started thinking about getting jobs. Ges Sydenham and Tony Willi had both decided to do A-Levels. Paul Reeve was thinking about going to Bath Lane Art College. Steve Baker had been offered a job as a plumber. I didn't have a clue what I was going to do but one thing I knew for certain was that I didn't want to go down the road that my dad had taken and end up in the shipyards.

GOOD TIMES, BAD TIMES

A JOB FOR LIFE?

On 2nd September 1974, I began my apprenticeship as a welder at Swan Hunter's Shipyard in Wallsend. Just like my dad had done twenty years earlier. During my final term at John Marley, I had sat down with the careers officer, who asked me what I wanted to do when I left school. She suggested that I answer the question as honestly as possible, and to base my answer on what I would like to do, regardless of whether or not I felt I had the necessary qualifications. I replied that I wouldn't mind being a singer and, if that didn't work out, I wouldn't mind giving acting a go. She laughed and told me, "Well, in the meantime, here's an application form for an apprenticeship for Swan Hunter Shipyards."

Two weeks later, I was invited to attend an interview at Swan Hunter's training centre in Wallsend.

The interview was conducted by Mr Craggs who, if I remember correctly, had only one eye. I imagined that he had lost his other eye in an accident in the yards; which was why, I assumed, he was now conducting interviews with the likes of me. I had no interest in shipbuilding and I hoped Mr Craggs would pick up on this and send me packing. He gave me a brief rundown of the history of Swan Hunter and asked me which of the various apprenticeships on offer I was most interested in. "Remember, whichever job you choose, there is a good chance you will be doing it for the rest of your working life so it's important that you make the right choice." Before I had the chance to explain that I didn't think I was cut out for a lifetime in the shipyards, Mr Craggs continued, "Based upon your exam results, and the fact that you did well in technical drawing, maybe you would be best suited to an apprenticeship as a draughtsman in our drawing offices."

I informed Mr Craggs that I would rather I had a job where I didn't have to come to work wearing a tie. He seemed a bit taken aback by this comment but handed me a list of blue collar apprenticeships that were available. I looked through the list of jobs. Sheet Metalworker. Plater. Caulker Burner. I liked the sound of none of them, and had no clue what they entailed, but there at the bottom of the list was Welder. At least I knew what a welder did. I told Mr Craggs I would like to be a welder. I still have no idea why I came to this decision: I hated metalwork at school, had no desire to work in the shipyards, and certainly had no desire to follow in my father's footsteps.

A couple of weeks after my interview, I received a letter offering me the opportunity to begin an apprenticeship as a welder at the 'world-renowned Swan Hunter Shipyards'. I showed the letter to my dad, hoping that he would try and talk me out of it as he had often remarked on what a shit job it was and how he wished that he had never become a welder. He read the letter, handed it back to me and said, "If that's what you want to do then go ahead and do it."

Each morning, I would be out of bed at six a.m., leave the house at six-thirty and walk the fifteen minutes up the West Road to catch the number 35 bus to Wallsend. The journey would take about half an hour. I would sit at the back of the bus, huddled in my ex-Navy greatcoat, my head resting against the window, and try to grab an extra few minutes' sleep. You had to be sure you were through the big metal gates in order to 'clock in' before seven-thirty as at that time they would come down and you would be locked outside. You would have to remain outside for fifteen minutes before the gates were raised and you were let in. Your pay would then be docked fifteen minutes. Many a time, the bus would be late getting to Wallsend and a whole load of us would jump off and run down the bank, throwing ourselves under the gates just as they were coming down. We knew that if you were late more than three times in any one week you would be suspended for a day without pay.

The flat rate of pay for an apprentice at that time was around forty quid a week. This could be supplemented by volunteering to work in the 'double bottoms' of the ships. The double bottoms, as the name would suggest, were in the bottom of the ship and if you volunteered to weld down there you were paid an extra fifty pence an hour 'confined space allowance'. On more than one occasion I had smelled burning and realised that my hair, held up in a hairnet under my welding helmet, had caught fire. I would fling my helmet to the ground and frantically put out my flaming hair. In the fire stakes, I would have given Arthur Brown a run for his money. Basically, I was being paid extra for ruining my health, not to mention my flowing locks. At the end of a shift in the double bottoms, I would emerge coughing up phlegm and my chest would ache like hell. But on the plus side, the 'gaffers' would very rarely venture down there, so for every hour I spent welding, I would spend another sleeping. Maybe it was something in the welding fumes. I always felt tired.

I hated working in the yards and I am sure my lack of interest would be reflected in the quality of my welding. It scares me to think that somewhere out there on the high seas there might be a ship that is being held together by my handiwork.

Some of the older guys I worked with had worked offshore with my dad and would often remark what a great bloke he was and how he was one for the birds. I would bite my lip when really I should have been telling them that I thought he was a total twat for behaving like he did when my mam was sat at home too scared to venture out, knowing that when he came home she would be getting the third degree as to what *she* had been up to while he had been away.

One night when my dad was back, we were sitting having our tea when the phone rang and my mam went to pick it up. She shouted, "Our Bobby, it's for you." When I picked up the phone there was a girl's voice I didn't recognise on the other end.

"Who are you?" I asked.

"We met up in Aberdeen, you gave me your number and asked me to call."

I realised it was not me that she was calling to speak to but my dad. I walked back into the kitchen and told him, "It's for you." My mam soon twigged what was going on and all hell broke loose. He said it was some girl in the office messing about, but my mam knew that he was lying. A massive shouting match ensued, where he tried to blame her for his infidelity.

The upshot of the argument was that my mam told him he had to move out. It was not the first time and she had always let him back in after a couple of days.

But this time it really did seem like he was gone for good. I felt sorry for my mam, and Suzanne also seemed upset that he had gone, but me and our Tony couldn't have been happier. We had spent many an hour in our room saying how we both wished he would just fuck off and leave. We had our wish.

My mam had a really tough time after my dad was gone and she became 'bad with her nerves' but she's a tough old girl and pretty soon seemed a lot happier than I had seen her in years. She even started going out and having a drink with Audrey, one of her mates from along the road. Drinking alcohol was something that my mam had never done when she was with my dad; she would stick to lime and soda. Now she enjoyed the occasional Bacardi and Coke.

One time, when she returned home after a night out, she came upstairs and told me and our Tony that she had brought a bloke back who she had met at Grey's Nightclub. He was waiting outside in his car; did we mind if he came in for a cup of tea? I told her, "You're not bringing any blokes in here. What are you thinking, wanting to bring some strange bloke in that you have just met at a nightclub?" She said OK and two minutes later we heard the car pulling away from outside our door. The next morning, we were sat having our breakfast when she told us that the bloke was Emlyn Hughes, the former Liverpool footballer. I was gutted. "Why didn't you say that last night? If I'd known, you could have brought him in; he might have given us some free tickets for the match."

Whether or not it really was the former Liverpool captain, I never found out, but I did feel guilty; it was her house, after all. Sorry, Mam!

ROCK AND ROLL

The only thing that got me through the working week was knowing that come Friday night I would be heading down to the Mayfair Ballroom in Newcastle. Wigan might have had its Casino and its Northern Soul but the true Soul of the North, as far I was concerned, could be found at the Mayfair on a Friday night. It was rock night and if you wanted to hear rock music played really loud, this was the place to be. Since I had started earning decent money, and reached the legal drinking age of eighteen, every Friday night at around ten o'clock me and my mates, many of whom also worked in the yards, would descend the red-carpeted steps into the Mayfair. At the sound of Led Zeppelin's *Rock and Roll*, along with a thousand kindred spirits I would hit the dance floor. We would each be giving our impersonation of Robert Plant or Jimmy Page.

Aside from the occasional journey to the bar for a pint of lager in a plastic glass, the dance floor was pretty much where you would stay until you filed out, drenched in sweat, at 2am. Then it was either a taxi home or pie and chips from the Barbecue Express at the top of Pink Lane. More often than not, pie and chips would win out before I'd start the long walk back to Whickham View.

I spent many Friday nights at the Mayfair with Hilary Clarke, the first girl that I ever fell in love with. Hilary came from Gosforth, an upmarket suburb on the outskirts of Newcastle. What she saw in me, a lad from Benwell, I was not sure, but pretty soon I was dating a 'posh lass'. On one of our first dates she took me to an Indian restaurant at the top of Northumberland Street. This was not only the first time that

I had been to a restaurant but also the first time that I would encounter Indian food. When the menu arrived, I didn't have a clue what to order so, rather than order the wrong thing, I decided to play it safe and ordered a bowl of boiled rice.

"Do you not want any curry with that?" Hilary asked.

"I'm allergic to curry so I'll just stick to rice, thanks."

That night, after I kissed Hilary goodnight and put her on the bus back to Gosforth, I headed off to the Barbecue Express for Saveloy dip and chips. I was starving.

Hilary was the first girl that I ever met who owned a horse. A budgie, a cat, or a dog, yes, but never a horse. Roller lived in a field just outside of Gosforth. I was terrified of that horse. I think he saw me as competition for Hilary's affection and he made his feelings obvious. I imagine horses, like dogs, can smell fear. Whenever I tried to get near, he tried to bite me. I'd had girlfriends in the past who had dogs that had taken a dislike to me, but this was the first time that I'd had to run away from a horse, being told, "Don't worry, he doesn't bite." But meeting Roller was not as scary as meeting Hilary's parents.

I was invited over for dinner at Hilary's house. The first thing I learned was that in Gosforth you had your dinner at tea-time and dinner-time was called lunch-time. When we sat down to eat, I was nervous as hell. Mr and Mrs Clarke sounded really posh and when I opened my mouth to speak, my Geordie accent sounded so broad that even I had difficulty understanding what I was saying. If I was trying to impress Hilary's parents, I don't think I did a very good job. I was certain that Mr and Mrs Clarke were more than a bit disappointed that their daughter was dating a long-haired character from Benwell, who worked in the shipyards. Ken in particular made it patently obvious that I was not the sort of bloke he wanted his daughter going out with. On all the occasions that I ventured up to Hilary's house, I don't think he ever spoke a single word to me, or looked me in the eye. I am sure Ken was a decent bloke and only wanted what was best for his daughter.

Hilary and I dated for around two years but broke up when she started seeing a guy who worked in the local Volvo garage. He also owned a car. What chance did I have? I didn't even have a driving licence. I was devastated.

In those two happy years before we broke up, if we were not at the Mayfair we would frequent another popular hang-out in Newcastle, the Jubilee (full name the Jubilee 77, to commemorate the Queen's Silver Jubilee). Before it was the Jubilee it was the Man in the Moon. It was here that I first heard the name of Bryan Younger.

Bryan Younger was a legend in the Man in the Moon. The word on the street was that he could play guitar like Jimmy Page from Led Zeppelin. If that was true, I had to meet this guy. I asked someone to point Bryan out to me and was directed to a darkened corner of the pub. There he sat, nursing a bottle of Double Maxim, with a fag hanging out of the corner of his mouth. He was dressed in a white Afghan coat and already had the makings of a full beard, which I was most impressed by; I could only dream of ever having a beard like that. I would later learn that Bryan was the same age as me, but he gave off an air of supreme confidence. Then again, with a beard and the ability to play like Jimmy Page, at the age of eighteen, who wouldn't be confident?

I walked up to Bryan, stuck out my hand and said, "I hear you can play guitar like Jimmy Page. Well, my name is Bob Smeaton and I can sing like Robert Plant." Could I sing like Robert Plant? Could I hell, but I knew that would get Bryan's attention. It seemed to work as, without looking up from his pint, he scribbled his address on a beer mat, handed it to me and said, "Come down to my place Tuesday night, let's see how good you are."

I turned up at Bryan's house on Springbank Road in Heaton. Bryan took me down the cellar, where he had his gear set up. He had two four-by-twelve cabinets and a Marshall amp. Lying against them was what looked like a Gibson Les Paul. Whether or not he could play like Jimmy Page, I was yet to discover, but he certainly had the gear. In the corner was a skinny, good looking kid with blond hair. He looked about thirteen and hadn't yet spoken a word. "This is Colin Roberts, my bass player," Bryan explained. Colin looked at me and nodded.

I stood at the microphone Bryan had set up in the middle of the room. Bryan turned to Colin and counted in: one, two, three. You would have had to be there to believe what happened next. Bryan and Colin, without pause for breath, played the whole of Zeppelin's first album. I knew the words to all of these songs so, even though I could not be heard over the noise that Bryan and Colin made, I sang along as best I could. Forty minutes or so later, in a wail of guitar feedback, Bryan ended *How Many More Times*.

"Well, what do you think?" asked Bryan, lighting up a fag.

"Brilliant," I replied.

"You didn't sound too bad yourself but you're going to need to buy a PA system."

"Am I in the band, then?"

"Yes," replied Bryan.

We were one member short of our line-up. Colin suggested that we look for a keyboard player but Bryan and I suggested that a drummer might be a better bet. Bryan said he knew this kid in Byker called John, who was playing in his brother's band but they had yet to do any gigs and he was keen to start earning some money.

John Miller might have been small but when he sat behind his kit he was transformed; he was the nearest thing to John Bonham I had ever heard. The night of our first rehearsal down in Bryan's cellar, we must have played every song that Led Zeppelin had ever recorded.

As John was packing away his kit, he asked us what we were called. At that point we didn't yet have a name. I suggested we called ourselves Heartbreaker, in honour of the Led Zeppelin song, but that we change the spelling so as not to be confused with another band that had just started doing the rounds, led by Tom Petty.

John asked when our next gig was.

"Soon, John," I replied, "soon."

HARTBREAKER

It would be easy for me to say that I saw the band as a way of getting out of the shipyards but I would be lying if I said that was the case. As much as I loved being in a band and being pointed out as I descended the stairs into the Man in the Moon as 'Bob Smeaton from Hartbreaker', it was still very much a sideline, and a break from the drudgery of being in the yards.

Having played our debut gig at the Wills Cigarette factory on the coast road during the summer of 1976, we started looking for gigs on the Newcastle pub circuit. We had decided we did not want to go down the route of playing working men's clubs: the clubs in our eyes were the death of a band. The pub circuit at the time, as far as we were aware, consisted of one pub, the Bridge Hotel. The Bridge was situated at the entrance to the High Level Bridge that crossed from Newcastle to Gateshead. To play a gig in the upstairs room on a Friday night would be an indication that we were getting somewhere.

One of the bands who had a regular Friday night slot at the Bridge was the Scratchband. The Scratchband were a bunch of blokes in their early thirties. To us, they seemed ancient. Our plan was to blow them off the stage and make the Friday night slot our own.

First, we had to convince them to give us a support slot, which we did by pointing out that by bringing along our followers, which at the time consisted of our girlfriends and a bunch of our mates, we could double their door takings. We also agreed to let them use our lighting rig: four catering-size coffee cans fitted with coloured light bulbs, operated by our roadies, Dave Duffy and Billy Anderson. We were not going to give Pink Floyd a run for their money but, having roadies and a lighting rig, we saw ourselves as serious contenders.

Our set list at the time consisted mainly of cover versions of popular rock songs, along with a couple of Elvis songs for good measure. Even though Elvis at this stage in his career was considered uncool, to me he was still The King and we would often end our set with *Jailhouse Rock* or *Hound Dog*. I was never able to convince the lads in the band to learn *Do the Clam*. Eventually, we also started dropping some of our own songs into our set. These sounded like copies of the bands that we loved. Our best song at the time was *Trouble on the Run*, which was pretty much a straight copy of a Free song.

Watch me spend my money
Watch me having fun
Watch me steal your love away
I'm Trouble on the Run

I'm Trouble on the Run
I'm Trouble on the Run
I don't care for nobody as long as I'm having fun

I wasn't going to be giving Bob Dylan any sleepless nights but we had started writing original songs and that gave us an advantage over the vast majority of the bands in the North East. But the mainstay of our set was covers of Zeppelin songs. We even went as far as having an acoustic section in our set as this is what Zeppelin did at the time. Bryan, Colin and I would pull out stools and perform pretty faithful renditions of *Going to California* and *That's the Way*. If you closed your eyes when we played the introductions to these songs, you could have imagined it was Zeppelin (that is, if they ever hit hard times and decided to play a gig at the Bridge Hotel). Until I started to sing. I was trying my best to sound like Robert Plant but I was failing miserably.

A couple of months after playing support at the Bridge Hotel, we started headlining. Now it was more than just our girlfriends and friends of the band who were coming to see us. One Friday night, we opened the doors to start letting the crowd in and the queue stretched down the stairs. The Bridge only held about 150 people but we must have crammed around 200 into the room that Friday night. We had sold out the Bridge Hotel. It was a milestone for the band.

At a number of our gigs, I saw a guy sitting in the audience who was a dead ringer for Brian Jones from the Rolling Stones. Following one gig, I noticed the same bloke was in deep conversation with Bry Younger. Bryan introduced us and, as it turned out, not only did he look like Brian Jones, he also played guitar. I could see what was coming next, and I was right. At the next rehearsal, there was Alan Fish. We ran through a number of songs and he could really play. His amp was turned up so loud it felt like my ears were going to bleed. It was bad enough trying to be heard over the noise of one guitar but two would be a real struggle. The thought of having him in the band did appeal, though. I could quite easily see him being Brian Jones to my Mick Jagger.

Alan started reeling off the names of some of the bands that he was into, such as the Allman Brothers and Little Feat. I noticed that they had one thing in common. Two guitarists and no frontman.

He also mentioned that he liked Focus. They didn't even have a singer and I thought, *I can see what's going to happen here: Alan in, Bob out.* But my fears were unfounded when I discovered that Alan and I shared a mutual love of the Who and we both agreed that *Waterloo Sunset* by the Kinks was the greatest pop song of all time. He also told me he thought I was a great frontman but that I just needed some better songs to sing; songs more suited to my voice. He went on to tell me that he wrote tunes but didn't write words. He played me some of the ideas that he had been working on and they were head and shoulders above what Bryan and I had been writing. Hartbreaker became a five-piece and me and 'Fishy' became the band's songwriters.

One day, we were having a band meeting in the City Tavern pub and we began discussing the idea that, as the line-up of the band had changed, maybe a change of name might be a good idea. John Miller suggested the name White Heat. I loved the James Cagney film of the same name and it had also been mentioned in a Velvet Underground song, *White Light, White Heat*. None of us were fans of the Velvets but we all liked the title. We told people that we had been approached by Tom Petty and the Heartbreakers' management and told we had to change our name. That was just bullshit, but it sounded good.

LOOK WHO'S BACK

I got back from work one night and my mam asked me to sit down as she had something to tell me. "Your dad is coming back."

I felt like she had punched me in the face. He had been away for almost two years and the thought of him coming back, and all the grief that him being home entailed, filled me with dread. My mam went on to explain that she was letting him come back as he had agreed to control his temper and he wasn't going to be 'working away' as he had got a job at home. The job he had was at Swan Hunters. I couldn't believe it.

The only upside I could see to him working in the same place as me was that I would no longer have to get the bus into work. I could travel in his car with him. Pretty soon, however, this became more like torture than a luxury. We would do the half-hour car journey in complete silence. He used to pick up his workmate on the way, who would sit in the front while I was consigned to the back. I might as well have not been there; I was never involved in their conversation. I started taking overtime shifts at work to avoid travelling back with him.

After my dad had been back for a couple of months, I could tell that not being able to go away to work was starting to get to him. I could also see that having him at home all the time was taking its toll on my mam. Pretty soon, he was back to picking on me again for the slightest thing. Any excuse and he would be in my face. The fact that I now had hair falling halfway down my back seemed to piss him off even more. When I would spend my time up in my bedroom listening to music, he seemed to take great pleasure in telling me that I was 'hippy lazy'. I once told him that I would like to go to America one day and he responded by telling me that they wouldn't let me in as they had enough hippies there already.

I was eighteen years old and as scared of him as when I was a child. The only difference now was that I had an idea as to why he behaved the way he did towards me. I felt it was because every time he looked at me it made him realise that he was not a young man anymore, and that caused some sort of resentment in him. I also felt he had regretted getting married and having kids when he was young and had not been able to live his life the way he wanted. But from my point of view he always did exactly what he wanted, and wasn't bothered about the effect it had on his family.

Eventually, I told my mam that I could no longer live at home. It was bad enough having to spend time travelling into work with him but to come home and be under the same roof was too much to bear. I took my Zeppelin and Sabbath posters off my bedroom wall, grabbed my albums and what clothes I needed, and moved into a flat with a workmate who lived about a mile away, on Ellesmere Road.

WHITE LIGHT WHITE HEAT

ABOUT THE YOUNG IDEA

By the time the long, hot summer of 1977 rolled around, I had already spent close to three years working in the shipyards. It wasn't getting any better. It was only the Friday nights at the Mayfair, along with the couple of gigs a week that I was playing with the band, that made life bearable. One lunchtime, rather than eat in the works canteen, I walked up the road to Wallsend High Street to check out the new releases in the record section of Woolworths. As I walked towards the counter there was a record playing that sounded familiar, but brand new at the same time. The guitar riff didn't sound a million miles away from what the Stones or the Who would have played; it was the singing that sounded different. I asked the girl behind the counter who it was and she told me it was *In the City* by a punk rock group called the Jam.

I had read about punk rock in the music papers but didn't pay it much attention, mainly because the groups were slagging off bands that I loved, like Zeppelin and the Eagles, calling them dinosaurs. But hearing the Jam single made me think that there might be something in this punk rock thing. I then heard the Clash's album and the Sex Pistols' first couple of singles, and had to admit that even though hearing those records didn't make me want to run out and cut my hair, there was something fresh and exciting in both the music and what they were singing about, that to be honest I hadn't heard on the last Zeppelin album.

I went to see the Jam at the Mayfair. Most of their songs seemed about two minutes long, and it was hard to tell where one ended and the next began, but anything they lacked in musical ability was more than compensated for by the energy of the band. They were brilliant.

Over the next six months, I went to see the Clash, the Damned, and the Buzzcocks. What I noticed was that the guys on stage were around the same age as me, whereas the guys in Zeppelin and the Eagles seemed ancient by comparison. Out of all the bands that I saw during that summer of punk, the Clash stood head and shoulders above the others. Joe Strummer, the lead vocalist, looked like he had been plugged into the mains circuit; he was frothing at the mouth. To me, he was like Elvis Presley; it looked like he had been beamed down from another world. The rest of the band were no slouches but I couldn't take my eyes off Joe. When I had been to see the likes of Robert Plant and Paul Rodgers on stage, they were like rock gods and seemed untouchable; I had never for one minute thought 'that could be me up there'. With Strummer, it was different. Give me a hair-cut and leather jacket, and a pair of skinny jeans, and that could have been me on that stage.

Following a Clash gig at Newcastle Polytechnic, I went back to my flat and looked in the mirror. I didn't want it to appear that I was jumping on the punk rock bandwagon but I knew that the hippy hair, crushed velvet shirt and flares had to go.

I didn't go the whole hog and cut off all of my flowing locks but soon my hair was cut to a respectable length. My trousers went through a similar pruning process, no longer falling over my desert boots but hugging my ankles above my 'brothel creepers'.

As much as Strummer made me take a long, hard look at my appearance, it was when I first heard the Elvis Costello album *My Aim is True* that the penny finally dropped. I was never going to be able to sing like Robert Plant or Ian Gillan, but I knew I was onto something when one night I was over at my mam's, playing the Costello album, when she asked, "Is that you singing?" She had never asked that when I was playing my Zeppelin albums.

It was also around this time that I began to progress as a frontman. I started to develop my own style; a hybrid of Mick Jagger and Joe

Strummer. Also, I was beginning to learn how to grab the attention of the audience by putting on a show. Halfway through a gig, I would take off my shirt and perform bare-chested. That would get the attention of the girls but because I was skinny the blokes in the audience would never feel intimidated. Even so, I would often drop to the floor and do press-ups, which would pump up what muscles I did have. I had an extra-long mic cable which would allow me to clamber into the audience. All these things were also a distraction from any bum notes that I might be singing. I never claimed to be the best singer in Newcastle but my reputation as a frontman was beginning to grow.

Alan Fish also acknowledged the wind of change that punk and new wave would bring and this started filtering through to our songs, which became shorter. My singing was more suited to this music. We didn't lose any of our original followers and even picked up a few new wave fans along the way. We were one of the few local bands at the time who had a large female following, and one thing I did know was that where there are girls, boys will follow. And that's pretty much what happened.

One of our regular gigs on the pub circuit was the Cooperage, on the Quayside in Newcastle. One night, after we finished playing and we were packing away our gear, we were approached by a really attractive blonde girl who introduced herself as Heather. She told us that she had seen the band a number of times and that tonight she had brought along her boyfriend, who had really liked us. I was quite surprised when she introduced him to us. He wasn't so much a boy but a man, in a suit and tie. I could see why Heather would have been attracted to him as he did have a look of Bryan Ferry about him, and a certain charm. As it turned out, he also shared the same Christian name as the Roxy Music frontman. He told us that he managed the record department of Windows music store and that he had his own record label, Rubber Records. He also mentioned that he was looking for a band to manage.

I was a bit wary of Brian Mawson. He didn't speak with a Geordie accent, in fact to my ears he sounded a bit posh. On the plus side, he did say that we were the best band that he had heard in years, and that he had connections at Impulse Recording studios in Wallsend and would be interested to hear what we sounded like on tape. It wasn't lost on me that a famous Liverpool band had also once been approached by a guy called Brian, who also managed a record shop and was offering his services as manager. What was good enough for the 'fab four' was good enough for us. Despite my initial reservations, Brian became the manager of White Heat. He also became one of my best friends; in fact, four years after we met, I was Best Man at his and Heather's wedding.

I thought that the band was ready to start looking for a record deal and that we should send off the demo tape that Brian had arranged for us to record at Impulse Studios. Brian told us we were not ready yet, that we should concentrate on building up our fan base in Newcastle, and wait for the record companies to come to us, rather than us go to them. We took on board what he suggested and began looking for more gigs around the North East. We were able to secure residencies at the Gosforth Hotel pub and also the Newton Park Hotel in Longbenton.

Phil Sutcliffe was a journalist for *Sounds* and came to see us at the Newton Park one Wednesday night during July 1978. Phil gave us our first review in a national newspaper. He raved about the band and suggested that the music we were playing was "music outside of categories", though doubtless a label would be made for it if we were to 'make it'. I cut out that review and kept it in my jacket pocket for months.

A NAIL IN MY HEART

Just as I began to feel that we were starting to get somewhere, our drummer John told us he wanted to leave the band. Brian Burness, who played in a local band called Kip, told me there was a guy called Geordie Waters who used to be in the band and who he felt would be a good fit for White Heat. As well as playing the drums, Geordie also had his own ice-cream business and ran a couple of vans up on the coast at Amble, which we thought would enhance our punk rock credentials. He looked like a young Tony Curtis, which we knew would appeal to the female members of our audience. When he sat behind his kit, we had no doubt he was the right man for the job.

Not long after Geordie joined the band, we heard it through the grapevine that *Bedrock*, the rock show that broadcast on BBC Radio Newcastle on a Monday evening, was looking to release a compilation album of local bands. We were sure that we would be included. We sent off our demo tape to Dick Godfrey, who was pulling the project together, and waited for our invitation. To say we were pissed off when we heard that we were not going to be included would be an understatement. Dick informed us that he didn't feel that we were quite ready yet but as a consolation we would be invited to appear at the Bedrock Festival that was being held over three days at the Newcastle Guildhall. At first we considered turning down the invite but realised that accepting would give us the chance to perform to our biggest audience to date. We also thought we would show the *Bedrock* people what they had missed by not including us on the album. We were second-bottom of the bill, below Hot Snax and Southbound, a couple of the bands who had appeared on the album.

By the time we hit the stage, we were spitting fire. We were about two songs into our set when a fight broke out in the crowd. I wasn't going to be upstaged by some idiots fighting. I jumped down, ran into the crowd and broke up the scrappers. I returned to the stage feeling pretty good about myself. Just as we were about to go into our next song, I noticed there was someone out there shouting abuse at the band. My adrenalin still pumping, I grabbed my mic and challenged whoever it was to "stop hiding in the crowd, be a man and come up here and say whatever it is you have got to say."

The audience parted like the Red Sea. Coming through the crowd was a giant of a man. I felt the blood drain from my face. I looked around to the other guys in the band for moral support, safe in the knowledge that at least there were five of us and only one of him. I was shocked to discover that my bandmates were already scurrying behind their amps. I heard Bryan Younger say, "Fucking hell, it's Jimmy the Nail." Now, at this moment in time I had no idea who 'Jimmy the Nail' was but anyone who looked like he did and went by the name of 'the Nail' was going to be really hard. He took the mic from my hand and bellowed, "What I would like to say is your band is shit." I wasn't going to argue. I think I might have even nodded in agreement. Jimmy handed me the mic and walked back into the crowd. We continued with the rest of our set and I am sure there was an extra quiver in my voice for the numbers that remained.

This was my first encounter with Jimmy the Nail but it would not be the last. Jimmy would become a regular at our gigs at the Newton Park Hotel. It would appear that Jimmy had in fact quite liked the band, and even went as far as to tell me that he thought I had a lot of bottle to stand up to him when he came on stage at the Guildhall. As much as Jimmy thought I was OK, for some reason he took a disliking to Brian Mawson. I could always tell whenever Jimmy had entered the room as Brian suffered from asthma, and the first sign of Jimmy would be the signal for him to pull out his asthma pipe and take a hit.

Jimmy the Nail would eventually form his own band, the King

Crabs, and approached Colin, our bass player, with an offer to join. Colin refused and told Jimmy that he was going to stick with White Heat as he felt we were a band that were going places, and that he didn't really fancy appearing on stage with a singer who would often turn up on stage wearing a woman's dress. Jimmy the Nail and his dress disappeared off the scene for a while and my thoughts were that he was probably doing a stretch in Durham Jail. Then one night, I was sat watching a programme on the telly called *Auf Wiedersehen, Pet* and there in one of the lead roles, playing a character called Oz, was Jimmy the Nail.

GIMME SHELTER

Having missed out on appearing on the *Bedrock* album, we were determined that the same thing was not going to happen with the *Sunday Sun Pop Awards*. The man behind the idea for the competition was Paul Nunn who, under the alias of Andy Bone, wrote a music column for the local Sunday paper.

It was announced that the winner was being promised a recording session with EMI and the added bonus was that the competition was being held at the Mayfair. The Mayfair was not only my favourite Friday night haunt but also where I had recently seen gigs by the Clash, the Jam and the Police.

We sent off our demo tape, along with a biography and an invite for Andy Bone to come along to see one of our gigs. Even before we had sent off our demo, we had a good idea that we would make the final four. We had a bit of an advantage over the other bands in that our manager Brian was quite friendly with Paul Nunn, who had already been to see us a couple of times. Not that we doubted that we deserved to be chosen but it helps to know a man on the inside. Sure enough, two weeks before the big night at the Mayfair, it was announced that White Heat would be joining Oasis (not *that* Oasis; in 1979 Liam Gallagher would have still been in short trousers and brother Noel would have yet to pick up a guitar), Burlesque, and the Piranha Brothers, at the final of the Andy Bone Pop Awards at the Mayfair on 6th April.

We were the third band to hit the stage and our crowd went nuts. I felt that their support, along with our showmanship and youthful enthusiasm, would be enough for us to be crowned the winners.

The last band to perform were the Piranha Brothers. They seemed to be a mix of comedy and song and I felt could well prove to be our biggest competition. Once they left the stage, there was a wait of around half an hour while the judges made up their minds. Andy Bone eventually walked on stage to announce the winners. The lads and I stood in the wings and waited for our name to be announced.

Andy stepped up to the mic. "The judges have come to a decision, and after much deliberation have decided that two bands should tie for first place. The winners are Oasis and White Heat. The prize is going to be shared between the two bands. Here's one of our judges, Alan Hull from Lindisfarne, to present the award to the winners." We were gutted that we hadn't won outright but at least we hadn't lost. We walked onstage, alongside the guys from Oasis, to receive the trophy from Alan Hull. I made sure I was the first to get my hands on it and I held it aloft in celebration. Then all hell broke loose.

The fans of Burlesque had decided that the competition had been fixed. They showed their disgust by pelting beer glasses at the stage. Luckily for us, the glasses were plastic; even luckier for Andy Bone, who was hit square in the face by one of the first glasses that was thrown from the crowd. It wasn't quite Altamont but it was getting nasty. I looked to the side of the stage, where I saw Brian Mawson gesturing to us to come off. I wanted to milk our moment in the spotlight but realised a speedy retreat was the best option.

As we left the Mayfair through the back door, we were greeted by two police vans with sirens screaming and blue lights flashing; two teams of Newcastle's finest boys in blue leapt out of the back of the vans and charged down the stairs. We had left at the right time. Ten minutes later, we were safely in the bar of the BBC club; a private club that Brian had become a member of, on New Bridge Street.

We were fortunate that none of the audience from the Mayfair or members of the other groups were present. If they had been, they would have noticed that Alan Hull, one of the judges, along with Andy Bone, had decided to join us for a drink. This would only have added fuel to the rumour that the competition was a fix. I sidled up to Alan

Hull and asked him if he had voted for us. He told me that he had, as he thought that we were the most original band in the competition. I was made up to be having a conversation with Alan Hull; he was the first famous person that I had ever properly met. I asked him if he had any advice, having just watched the band on stage. He told me that the most important thing was to write songs about what you know and where you come from. He said that everyone had a story to tell that was exclusive to them, and that's what people wanted to hear. He pointed out that *Fog on the Tyne* and *Run for Home* were both written about Newcastle but had still found an audience outside of the North East, and had gone on to become two of Lindisfarne's biggest hits.

As our conversation progressed, I learned that Alan, like me, had been brought up in Benwell and that even though he had done a number of jobs outside of music, he had only ever wanted to be a musician. I told him that I worked in the shipyards and how much I hated it, especially having to get out of bed at six in the morning. At this point in the conversation he suddenly got serious and told me that I could not be serious about making it as a musician if I had the safety net of a regular job, and that no musician gets out of bed before ten o'clock. I thought to myself that was easy for him to say, having had a string of hit records.

By the time we left the BBC club, it was daylight. I staggered home with the winners' trophy in my hand and Hully's words ringing in my ears.

HELL BENT FOR LEATHER

White Heat might have won the competition at the Mayfair but there was still no sign of the prize of a recording session. Maybe Oasis had got the studio time, seeing as I had nabbed the winners' trophy, which now had pride of place on my mantelpiece.

When I sat down to eat my tea one Wednesday evening, it had been six weeks since the competition and there was still no word from EMI as to when we might be invited to record at their studios in London. After another shitty day at work, I tried my best not to sound too miserable when I answered the phone and Brian Mawson asked me the same question he had a hundred times before: "What are you up to tonight?"

"Not a lot," I replied, "I'm not up for a drink, I think I might just stay in and watch the telly."

"No, you won't. Get changed and get yourself down to the City Hall. You're playing there tonight, supporting Judas Priest."

My initial reaction was 'fucking hell, we're going to be playing the City Hall'. My second thought was, 'holy shit, the fans of Judas Priest are going to hate us'. Judas Priest were an out-and-out heavy metal band; we would be like lambs to the slaughter. But on the other hand, we were local lads, which I thought might count in our favour, and we were still in essence a rock band, even though we'd been bitten by the new wave bug.

We arrived at City Hall and sat down in the empty auditorium while Judas Priest were finishing their sound check. One of their road crew instructed us to set up our gear at the front of the stage. We were told that we could only do a quick sound check as the doors would be opening in ten minutes. I looked down from the stage to row D, seat 22. Tonight someone else would be in that seat where six years earlier I had sat and watched my first-ever gig.

This felt like the big time. We were given a dressing room backstage and waited until the clock rolled around to eight, when we were told we had to be on stage for our half-hour support slot. I don't remember much about the gig itself but I do remember that when I introduced *Wish I Could Dance*, one of our newest songs, someone in the audience shouted out, "I wish you could sing." It was good to see that the Geordie faithful had not lost their sense of humour. I also remember that at one point I jumped down from the stage and walked across the backs of the seats to stand on the back of what I hoped was seat D22. I turned around and looked at my band, White Heat, on stage at Newcastle City Hall.

After the gig, we were in our dressing room when in walked Rob Halford, the lead singer of Judas Priest. Rob was dressed head-to-toe in his leather stage outfit. I thought he looked a bit daft but he seemed like a really nice guy and nothing like the wild man he portrayed on stage. Twenty years later, Rob came out of the closet and announced he was gay but back in 1979 we had no idea. He handed us a bottle of wine and told us, "Well done, lads, I look forward to seeing more of you on the rest of the tour." The next night we were back at the City Hall, then the tour would take us to Sheffield City Hall before hitting Judas Priest's home town of Birmingham and finally ending at London's Hammersmith Odeon.

By the time we reached Sheffield, we were getting used to playing on the bigger stages and also choosing songs that we felt were best suited to winning over a partisan audience. After the show, we headed to the Limits Club, Sheffield's number-one hotspot. One of Priest's road crew told me how much he liked White Heat. He explained that at the gigs so far he had kept the volume down to number five, in order to hold back for when Judas Priest came on stage but that at the next gig, in Birmingham, he was going to give us the benefit of the whole of the PA system. He also told us that his mate, the lighting technician, would be pushing up a few extra faders when we came on stage.

We had been in the club for around an hour or so when we noticed there was a bit of a commotion at the entrance. Rob Halford had arrived, with a couple of guys from the band. Rob had switched out of his stage gear into a new outfit, still retaining the black leather look. He and the guys were given a table in the VIP area and after a few minutes one of the staff at the club came over to tell us that Rob had invited us to join him. Great, we thought, we get to hang out with the Priest. Pretty soon, we were helping ourselves to the complimentary booze but, aware that we had a gig to do the following night, we decided we'd better start thinking about heading back to the hotel. Our bass player Colin was deep in conversation with Rob and, as he got up to leave, Rob suggested he should stay a bit longer. Colin, who'd had a few drinks by this point, responded by taking his backstage pass off his jacket and sticking it on Rob's forehead. We didn't hang around long enough to see if Rob had seen the funny side of this.

The next morning, we were having breakfast when Brian Mawson walked into the room and told us that we were no longer on the tour and that we would be heading back to Newcastle. We were shocked. The reason given was that the tour promoters had decided that for the show in Birmingham they were going to bring in a local band for the support slot. We had our own ideas. Maybe Judas Priest had got wind of what the road crew had up their sleeve for Birmingham, or Rob Halford had taken offence at Colin's response to his invite to 'stay a little bit longer' at the Limits Club. Whatever the reason, we were on our way back to Newcastle. But we had shown that we could now compete with the 'big boys'.

WE GOTTA GET OUT OF THIS PLACE

I had just scrambled under the shipyard gates before they closed when I was handed my time card. I was also handed a white envelope. It looked like once again I was going to be suspended for bad time-keeping. I opened the envelope and couldn't believe what it said.

We regret to inform you that due to a downturn in the demand for ships, Swan Hunter Shipyards are looking to make redundancies. Before any compulsory redundancies are made, we are looking for volunteers. Those who volunteer will receive three months' pay in lieu of notice.

Everyone was walking around reading the same letter. Some blokes were close to tears; others, like my mate Mick Attridge, were waving the letter in the air like they had just been told that they had won the pools. Like me, Mick hated working in the yards. He told me he was going to take redundancy and use the money to travel the world. He suggested that I do the same.

As I was getting my welding gear out of my locker, my head was spinning. I went off and found my gaffer and asked him what he thought I should do. He said, "Bob, take the redundancy. If you don't take it, they'll probably make you redundant, regardless. They will get rid of those who have been here the least amount of time and those who have bad time-keeping records." I fell into both of those categories.

This was my chance to get out of the yards and be paid for the privilege. I had to ask myself, did I think the band were going to make it? We were still not earning a lot of money and had yet to secure the elusive recording contract but maybe my leaving the yards and becoming a full-time musician would help give us that extra push that was needed. What was it that Alan Hull had said? You could not be serious about being a musician while holding down a full-time job. Even if the band didn't achieve the sort of success that I was hoping for, a life working in the yards was never really going to be an option. There wasn't a great amount of soul-searching required as to whether or not I felt I was doing the right thing. Later that same morning, I went back to my gaffer and told him I wanted to volunteer to be made redundant.

After work that night, I went over to my mam's to break the news. She couldn't believe that I was quitting my job. While she was giving me a bollocking and telling me that I had done the wrong thing, my dad sat there and didn't say a word. I couldn't believe it; I expected him to go mad with me and tell me what an idiot I was, and that if I thought that being in a band was any way to earn a living, I had another thing coming. Instead, silence.

Two weeks later, I was given my last-ever pay packet from Swan Hunter. Inside it was four hundred quid, the most money I had ever had in my life. They were paying me to leave the place.

As it turned out, it wasn't just me who left the yards that summer of 1979. My dad left also. He wasn't offered redundancy; he quit and took a job up in Scotland. It seemed like he was hankering to get back to his old tricks again. One night, without any fanfare or tears, my mam said they were splitting up for good.

I was out of the shipyards, it looked like my dad was out of my life, and I had four hundred quid in my pocket. Within a week, I met a bloke who would change my life.

Geoff Wonfor was a giant of a man, both in size and personality, and the funniest and kindest man that I would ever meet. He was also the first man that ever told me he loved me. When Brian Mawson first introduced me to Geoff, in the Portland pub next to the BBC studios on High Bridge Street, where Geoff worked as a television director, Geoff was in the process of asking Brian if he could lend him a couple of quid to buy a packet of fags. I pulled Geoff to one side and told him that I had just taken redundancy from my job at the shipyards, had been paid four hundred quid, and could lend him some money. Geoff refused the offer but told me many years later that he never forgot that moment and how I was prepared to lend some money to someone that I had just met. If he had taken me up on my offer of a loan of a hundred quid, in the years that followed he would have paid it back a thousand times over. That first meeting, as they say in the movies, was the beginning of a beautiful friendship.

Geoff was mates with the guys in Lindisfarne and had recently made a couple of promotional films for them. He had also been able to get these promo films shown on the BBC's local news programme. Brian Mawson suggested to Geoff that he come down and check out White Heat, in the hope that he would like us enough to make a promo film for us.

Geoff came along to see the band the following week at a gig we were playing at Balmbra's Music Hall in Newcastle's Bigg Market. After the gig, Geoff told us that we were the best band that he had seen since the Rolling Stones. As I would discover over the years, Geoff was a man for exaggeration, but on this occasion I was not going to argue with him. He then started telling us his plans to get us on the telly. But first we had to get a record out.

NERVOUS BREAKDOWN

My song-writing partner, Alan Fish, had just written a guitar riff that he thought was really strong and that, with the right words, could be a potential single. He suggested that I write some lyrics about having a nervous breakdown. I am sure that this was a suggestion on Alan's behalf as to my state of mind at the time. I wrote some words and when they were married to Alan's guitar riff we felt it was the best song that we had ever written. When we first performed the song live, by the time we had finished its debut performance our audience were already singing along to the chorus.

During the guitar solo, I would drop to the floor and do ten push-ups. This was an indication of the effect of new wave on the band: two years earlier, the guitar solo would have required a hundred push-ups.

One night during October 1979, we arrived at Impulse Studios in Wallsend and played the song to the engineer Mickey Sweeney, who was going to produce the sessions. Mick said it was the best guitar riff that he had ever heard. He loved it so much that he wanted to use it as the chime on the bell of his front door. It was only two notes but it was catchy as all hell.

As yet, our attempts to get any record company big wigs to leave London and come to Newcastle to see the band had been futile. We had been offered a couple of London gigs but didn't want to go down there and play to one man and his dog. Brian Mawson suggested that we release *Nervous Breakdown* as an independent single, on our own record label. We knew that this would sell well in the North East, which might make the record companies in London sit up and take notice; even get off their arses and make the journey up to Newcastle to see the band on our home turf.

We decided to call our label Vallium, which we felt was quite apt for a song called *Nervous Breakdown*. Once we had recorded and mixed the song, I went along to watch the pressing of the single. I remember holding it in my hand and thinking it was the most beautiful thing I had ever seen.

We didn't want to have a photo of the band on the sleeve and thought instead we would have something that tied in with the subject matter of the song. It was decided that the sleeve should feature someone having a nervous breakdown. Our drummer Geordie volunteered and we thought it would be a good idea for him to have his nervous breakdown in the middle of Northumberland Street, the busiest street in Newcastle. Bry Younger and I were going to be the white-coated doctors who would attend to George while he was having his 'turn'.

Rik Walton, a local photographer, had volunteered to take the shot for us and managed to capture the moment just as two policemen arrived on the scene. The picture made the front of the sleeve, which we folded ourselves. We included a thank you to the Boys and Girls for supporting the band since 1977. The 'Hooray Boys and Girls' was the name that we had given to our followers who, upon their approval of a worthy performance, would spontaneously break into a chant of 'Hooray, Hooray'.

Leading up to Christmas, we had the best-selling single in the North East. Our sales were helped thanks to Geoff Wonfor, who was true to his word and filmed us miming to the track, and was able to get the clip shown on the local BBC news programme. When the single was reviewed in *Sounds*, the guy who reviewed it said that had it not been for the Jam releasing *Eton Rifles* that same week, he would have chosen *Nervous Breakdown* as single of the week.

As 1979 rolled into 1980, we started getting plays on the John Peel show. John loved the record and would often play it two or three times a week. I think he might have also been attracted to the song because my vocals had a hint of the Fergal Sharkey tremble about them, and the Undertones were one of his favourite bands. The spirit that was captured in *Nervous Breakdown* was not a million miles away from the Undertones' *Teenage Kicks*.

Steve Wright also gave us a play on his show on Radio One, playing it back-to-back with Elvis Costello's *Oliver's Army*, and noting the similarity between the two songs. One of the guys who worked in Listen Ear, one of the local record shops that were selling the single, told me that Elvis Costello had called in and picked up a copy of *Nervous Breakdown*. I hope he took my vocal performance as flattery rather than plagiarism.

Pretty soon, we started picking up sales around the rest of the country and reached number two in the independent charts. The single was hovering just outside the top fifty of the national charts but by the time we started picking up sales around the UK, sales in the North East had started tapering off. We would have loved to appear on *Top of the Pops* and if we had I am sure *Nervous Breakdown* would have been a massive hit.

Thanks to the wonders of the internet you can now Google 'White Heat, *Nervous Breakdown*' and get an idea of what the TV audience around the country had missed out on.

Many years later, it was covered by a Canadian Band called the Tranzmitters and, strangely enough, also by an Asian group called First Alert. You can see and hear First Alert's interpretation of *Nervous Breakdown* on YouTube. The lead singer even went as far as copying my vocal style but judging from the clip he didn't attempt the push-ups.

While *Nervous Breakdown* was outselling every other single in Newcastle, the reps from the major record companies would ask the dealers in the shops how well the records on their label were doing. They would be told they were doing OK but were being outsold by a local band called White Heat. The reps would report this to their bosses at the labels back in London. They had to sit up and take notice of what was happening in Newcastle. Our cause was also massively helped when a guy called Ian Ravendale came to see us at Balmbra's and gave us a review in *Sounds*.

"White Heat have got it here now, right this moment, they are as arresting as anything that is currently shifting albums by the furniture van full, everything about them screams 'Yes'."

He ended his review with an invite to the record companies in London:

"The first Newcastle train leaves King's Cross at precisely one a.m."

They finally began to get the message.

On one particular night, we had people from Virgin, CBS and EMI in the crowd at the same time. Pretty soon, we had a number of offers on the table. I would have signed the first recording contract that was put in front of me, even if it included a clause that said I had to clean the offices and make the tea. I was desperate to be signed. Brian Mawson, however, told us to be cautious and not to rush into anything.

The first contract that we were happy with was offered by Virgin music. The guy who ran the publishing arm of Virgin was an Australian called Laurie Dunn. I really liked him and he seemed like someone I could trust. Brian felt the same way and in March 1980 we signed a deal with Virgin Music Publishing. With the cheque in the bank, the next thing was for the rest of the guys in the band to quit their day jobs. White Heat were no longer a bunch of electricians, butchers and ice-cream sellers. We were full-time musicians

MAKING FRIENDS WITH THE MEN IN THE FUNNY SUITS

As 1980 got underway, I started to believe that I was going to 'make it'. In fact, I had honestly started thinking that White Heat were going to be as big as the Rolling Stones. Not that I would have mentioned this to anyone at the time, not even the other lads in the band. They would have thought that I was going mad. I saw Bob Dylan interviewed many years later. He said he always felt it was his destiny that he was going to succeed but he kept this feeling to himself for fear that if he voiced it, other people would crush it. These words resonated with me. That's how I felt. I had felt so differently three years previously, when the band was just a side-line to my day job, but now all the pieces seemed to be falling into place. I looked at the other bands who were 'making it', such as U2 and Simple Minds, and I honestly thought that we could give them a run for their money. We had the songs, a loyal and vocal following in the North East, and I felt it was just a matter of time before our success on home soil would be repeated on a national level.

We were on first-name terms with most of the people who came to see us. We would chat to them before and after the gigs and they wanted to know everything that was happening with the band. Had we signed a record deal yet? When would we be recording an album? Had we written any new songs?

Having such a loyal following was a blessing and a curse. It was great that they had such a vested interest in the band but I felt under pressure not to let them down. White Heat had to succeed for them as much as for ourselves.

The thing about people in the North East is their loyalty. If they get behind you, they will stick with you through thick and thin. It's the same with the football team. Even during hard times, St James' Park is still packed to the rafters for every game.

A great deal of the band's success to date was down to that type of loyalty. Our audience wanted something to get behind, something to cheer for. White Heat were 'their band' in the same way that Newcastle United were 'their team'. Many of our followers had regular jobs similar to what the guys in the band had before we had gone 'full-time'. A number of them had been following us since we played our first gigs at the Bridge Hotel back in 1976. I would see many of them either at the match or out having a drink on a night out on the Toon. Watching football and coming to see the band was their escape. It had been the same for me but now I was the guy up on stage in the band.

We landed a gig supporting the Climax Blues Band at The Venue in London. When our fans in Newcastle got wind that we were playing a Saturday night gig in the 'big city' they decided to hire a bus to come down and lend their support. The Venue held around fifteen hundred people and doubled as both a nightclub and live music venue. It was owned by Richard Branson as another part of his expanding Virgin empire. Back in 1981, Branson was not the high-profile figure that he is today but he was the owner of Virgin Records and had the power to decide if his label would sign a band or not. We had been told that he might well be attending the gig, having heard good reports about us.

Once we hit the stage, it was evident that most of the audience were only there to see the Climax Blues Band. It would appear that they were more interested in eating their suppers than watching the support band. I knew we had our Newcastle contingent on side; it was those people who were ignoring us that we had to win over. I charged across the dance floor to the tables where they were sat and trampled on their burgers. I am not sure this totally endeared me to them but it did result in one journalist who was there to review the gig starting his review with the strapline: "Waiter there's a boot in my dinner".

Our fans had travelled all the way from Newcastle and spent their hard-earned cash in doing so, and it would be five a.m. before they got back home. The least we could do was put on a show for them and not go down without a fight. I believe we did that. To use a football term, we might not have won three points but we were playing away and would be returning home with a respectable score draw. We had not let our fans down.

After the gig, we headed upstairs to the dressing room and were towelling ourselves down when in walked a bearded hippy-looking guy. I thought he was a member of the Climax Blues Band coming in to congratulate us on our performance. As it turned out, it was Richard Branson. He started telling us how he had heard great reports about the band from Laurie Dunn and that he had really enjoyed the gig. I said, "OK then, Richard, we get what you're saying but when are you going to sign us to your label?" He picked up a felt-tip pen from the table and signed his name across my bare chest. "There you go, I've signed you."

Branson was true to his word and within a week we received a contract for the band to sign. White Heat were now signed to Virgin Music Publishing *and* Virgin Records.

TALES FROM THE TOWNHOUSE

One of the perks of signing with Virgin was that they owned residential recording studios. As well as recording there, you could live on the premises. One of these was the Manor Studios in Oxfordshire, where Mike Oldfield had recorded *Tubular Bells*. Another was the Townhouse Studios, on Goldhawk Road in Shepherd's Bush. We started living and recording at the Townhouse. What we didn't realise at the time was that even though Virgin owned the studio, they were not giving us it for free. All the recording time and cost of staying there was going on our bill and would be recouped against future record royalties.

At the time I was living in the penthouse suite. It was twice the size of the flat that I was sharing with my mate back in Newcastle. I would come down in the morning and me and the rest of the lads in White Heat would have our breakfast with the other bands who were recording there.

One artist who was at the Townhouse was a famous drummer who was recording his first solo album during a break from his regular band. I would hear his drums blasting down the corridor. I had never heard drums sound like that before. I got friendly with the famous drummer's roadie and would chat to him about how the recording was going. One evening, as the drum roadie was leaving, I said, "See you tomorrow."

He replied, "I'll be back soon, I'm just off to get [the famous drummer's] gear."

An hour or so later, he returned.

"Did you get his gear?" I asked.

"Yeah, would you like to try some?"

Now, this is where I got a little bit confused. Why would I want to try a snare drum or a hi-hat, or whichever piece of gear the roadie had been dispatched to retrieve? But I thought: in for a penny, in for a pound. "Yeah, that would be great." I had no idea what I was in for.

The roadie and I went off to a cupboard, where he dug into his pocket and pulled out a wrap of paper then chopped out a line of white powder. So this was the famous drummer's 'gear'. I watched as the roadie rolled up a tenner and sniffed the gear up his nose. I was a quick learner and did the same.

My experience with drugs up to this point had been confined to the great boot polish robbery of 1973, a bit of weed, and one disastrous acid trip. But this was cocaine; the drug of choice for the rich and famous. I was not yet rich or famous but if this was going to help me on my way, I was up for it. Having had a line of 'gear' I then went up to the games room, where my bandmates were having a game of pool. I have never been a great pool player but I entered the game and cleared the table of all the balls, and then for the next twenty minutes recounted to anyone who would listen how great I had become as a pool player.

We had just about finished the album and were well into the mixing stage when I was told that I was going to have to vacate the penthouse suite as Ozzy Osbourne was going to be using the studio as his London base. I wasn't going to begrudge Ozzy the use of the penthouse suite. He was a legend.

We didn't see him around the studio until one night when we were all sat in the control room, having a few celebratory drinks while listening to a playback of our finished album. The studio door burst open and in he walked, having no doubt heard that there was a bit of a party happening in Studio 2.

Ozzy instructed our producer, Simon Boswell, to turn up the music. Simon was not going to argue and pushed the fader on the desk up to its limits. The speakers were nearly jumping off the walls. Ozzy started headbanging along to the tracks. I couldn't believe it - this was Ozzy fucking Osbourne! It was his image from the sleeve of *Black Sabbath Volume 4* that I had painted onto my school haversack, when I was first getting into 'hairy music'. It looked like we had Ozzy's seal of approval. Once we'd finished listening to the album, Ozzy suggested we should all retire to O'Donoghue's, the Irish pub next door.

When we entered the pub, a Ceilidh band was in full swing. We found a table near to where the band was playing and, to get into the spirit of things, ordered a round of Guinness. It was going down a treat and we were all feeling a little melancholy as the band began to play a mournful version of *Danny Boy*, a song that was always guaranteed to tug at the old heart strings. We were almost at the point of weeping into our drinks when Ozzy got to his feet and requested that the band give us a rendition of *Paranoid*. Now, they were a good band but I had no doubt that their repertoire didn't include the Sabbath classic. The pub and the band fell silent. I suggested we make a hasty retreat back to the Townhouse before any further pressure was put on the already fragile Anglo-Irish relations.

In the safety of Ozzy's penthouse suite, the party continued in earnest. Simon Boswell's girlfriend, Dot, had joined us for the playback of the album and had brought along with her one of the first-ever Polaroid cameras, which were a bit of a novelty at the time. Ozzy took a shine to Dot's camera and pretty soon he and the camera disappeared. An hour or so must have gone by when we noticed that the camera was sat there on the table in the middle of the room, with a recently-taken photograph hanging out and still drying. Dot picked up the camera as an image magically appeared, of a hand holding a penis. As Ozzy was the last person to be seen with the camera, he was the prime suspect. When the charge was put to him by Dot, Ozzy pleaded his innocence, to which Dot replied, "Well, it's either yours or you're holding someone else's."

Across the knuckles of the hand was tattooed the name 'Ozzy'.

SPRINGSTEEN AND ME

At the time we were recording our album, I was obsessed with Bruce Springsteen. I had come late to Springsteen, and first heard *Born to Run* around the end of the 1970s, a couple of years after its 1975 release. But once I started listening to him, I listened to very little else. His double album *The River* had been released a couple of months before we had commenced recording. During the time we were in the studio, I had a cassette of the album and played it incessantly. I would play it first thing in the morning, before we started our sessions, and last thing at night, before I went to bed. The other lads in the band would come into my room and say, "Bloody hell, Bob, not Springsteen again." I loved that record so much, if White Heat could have got anywhere near the sound that Springsteen got on that album, I would have been happy. We even went as far as to recruit the saxophone player John 'Irish' Earle, a member of Graham Parker's band the Rumour, to play on a number of the songs on the album. Irish had played on Thin Lizzy's *Dancing in the Moonlight*, which also owed a lot to Springsteen. I saw Irish as taking on the Clarence Clemons role in White Heat.

Despite loving what Bruce had released on record, I had yet to see him live. This was set to change when, at the back end of 1980, I bought tickets to see him at Newcastle City Hall, during March of the following year. As it turned out, when March rolled around, we were in the middle of recording our album. It looked like I was going to have to miss the gig. But then Bruce got sick and had to rearrange the concert. The date was rescheduled for 11ᵗʰ May. By then, our album was just about finished and I would be able to make it back to the Toon for the gig.

In the weeks leading up to the concert, I began telling my mates that Bruce had re-scheduled the date so that I would be able to make it, and also that he and I had arranged to do a duet at the show. This was of course total bullshit, but it always got a laugh.

My then-girlfriend Angela and I had great seats, about five rows from the front. Springsteen came on stage and started his set with *Follow that Dream*, an Elvis Presley song. Even before the first song was over, it was already the greatest gig that I had ever seen.

About five songs into the set, the band started playing *Tenth Avenue Freeze-Out* and halfway through the song Bruce jumped offstage and started walking on the backs of the seats. I couldn't believe it but it looked like Bruce was heading my way. The next thing I knew, he was standing on the seat right in front of me. This almost felt like a dream. I had been overdosing on Springsteen in the weeks leading up to the show and I expected any minute to be woken up by my alarm clock, to start another day of recording at the Townhouse. Whether or not this was a dream, I knew what was coming next. I was going to sing a duet with Bruce. And that is what I did. I heard my voice alongside Bruce's, blasting out of the PA system. It was Bruce Springsteen, Bob Smeaton, and the E Street Band.

At the end of the song, Bruce shook my hand and said, "Hey, you know that sounded pretty good." I don't recall much about the rest of the first half of the gig but when the band took their break I headed off to the foyer, where I bumped into my sister Sue, who was at the show with her boyfriend. Although she hadn't actually seen me doing my duet with Bruce, she said that halfway through the song she turned and said to her boyfriend, "Bloody hell, that's our Bob singing with Springsteen."

For weeks following the gig, people were coming up to me saying they thought I'd been taking the piss when I'd said I was going to sing with 'the Boss'. I would reply by saying that the gods were smiling down on me that night. This might all sound a bit Walter Mitty and to this day I would still find it hard to believe, had Angela not taken a photograph at the precise moment that Bruce and I were in full voice. Many years later, a bootleg tape of the concert appeared and there, during *Tenth Avenue Freeze-Out*, is my duet with Springsteen. I must admit, it sounded better on the night.

IN THE ZERO HOUR

Prior to releasing our album, it was decided that we would release another single. To promote this, we had lined up a tour support slot with the Vapours, who were riding high in the charts with their single *Turning Japanese*. Just prior to starting the tour, Geordie Waters told us that he wanted to leave the band so John Miller, our previous drummer, re-joined us.

When the tour was over, we were offered another support spot, with a band called Adam and the Ants, who were being tipped for great things. We decided against it as we didn't think that they would pull the crowds. Six months later, they were number one and the biggest band in the country. Rather than playing to crowds of screaming girls, we were sat at home in Newcastle, planning our next move.

Our next move was to release our album. I would make regular visits down to the Virgin offices in Ladbroke Grove, to try and get an idea of what was happening. One afternoon, I was sat in the office when one of the A&R people at Virgin came in and started chatting to me about White Heat and how things were going.

"Great," I replied, "I just wish we could get the album out, we've been writing a bunch of new songs and almost have enough material for our second album."

The conversation moved on to Malcolm Owen, who had been the lead singer in the Ruts but had died of a heroin overdose a few months earlier. The A&R guy asked me what I thought of the Ruts, who were another of Virgin's bands, then asked me if I would be interested in joining them as their lead singer. I couldn't believe what he was saying. Why would he be asking me to leave White Heat to join another band? This was the label who were supposedly behind us. Alarm bells started to ring. Something was wrong here.

It transpired that Laurie Dunn had recently had a fall-out with the people at Virgin; also, Phil Collins, who had just released his first solo album *Face Value*, had become a massive seller and the label were using the money from the success of that album to sign a load of new bands.

It felt like we were no longer a priority for the label; we found ourselves at the back of the queue. We had signed the deal with Virgin but it now looked like they were not going to release our album.

We decided to buy back the tapes of the album from Virgin and release it on our own label. *In the Zero Hour* was released in December 1981. Our loyal following made it the best-selling album in the North East, where we were top of the album charts that Christmas, but I couldn't see where we were going to go from there.

One evening during January 1982, the band got together with our manager, Brian, to discuss what the future held for White Heat. To be honest, it didn't look that bright. We couldn't go chasing another record deal, we were always going to be damaged goods. Whichever way we looked at it, we knew that the game was up. To use another football analogy, personally I was never going to be happy with White Heat being a mid-table team; that was never going to be enough for me. If we were not fighting for the title, I couldn't see the point. We didn't want to let the thing fizzle out. If we were going to bow out, it was going to be in a blaze of glory.

Brian said that we had to plan a big show for what would be our farewell concert. The problem was, we had pretty much outgrown gigs like Balmbra's and the Newton Park. Brian said we should book the Mayfair Ballroom. No local band had ever sold out the two-and-a-half-thousand capacity venue without a record in the national charts but Brian was convinced that we would be the first. The date was set for the following month, Friday 26th February.

When we broke the news to Geoff Wonfor that the band was breaking up, he was close to tears. Geoff had championed White Heat for the past three years and the film clips that he had made for us which had been shown on local television were instrumental in the success that we had enjoyed. If Brian was the sixth member of the band, Geoff was the seventh. He told us he could convince the producers of *Check It Out* - an arts show on Tyne Tees Television - that we deserved to have a half-hour special made. Tyne Tees had never afforded a local band that sort of coverage before but Geoff was certain he could do it. The problem for Tyne Tees was that he was working for the BBC at the time. Geoff said he would direct the programme for free. He was a hard man to argue with and, by sheer strength of will, he won them over. Tyne Tees were on board and Geoff was going to direct the documentary.

Geoff filmed our penultimate gig, at the Gulbenkian Studios. We played a full set of songs and also mimed to most of the songs from our album. Geoff also took me down to the Swan Hunter shipyards and filmed a sequence there. Going back was scary and I dreaded the thought that, with no band, I might have to return to work there one day. I put that thought to the back of my mind. The whole of the White Heat *Check It Out* special has subsequently appeared on YouTube. One of my quotes in the documentary was that I didn't want to be Bob Smeaton who used to be in White Heat, I wanted to be Bob Smeaton who is, or who is going to be. Watching it now, it's hard not to laugh, but that was how I felt at the time, and I can see why people might have thought I was being big-headed and that I sounded like a bit of a twat. But I looked great and I had a shed-load of youthful arrogance.

The *Check It Out* special was broadcast a week before our final gig. The day after it aired, Brian called to say that the gig was a sell-out. In the week leading up to it, people who had never seen White Heat in performance were stopping me in the street and asking me why the band was splitting up. That was the power of television. I am certain that if we had received this sort of coverage on a nationwide basis, we wouldn't have been throwing in the towel.

Finally, the night of the last performance rolled around. Steve Farrier, a mate of mine who I used to work with in the yards, picked me up in his Jaguar and dropped me outside the Mayfair. I remembered that it was five years earlier when Hartbreaker had first sold out the Bridge Hotel and I had climbed the stairs past two hundred people, thinking 'bloody hell, we might be onto something here'. Now I was walking down the red-carpeted stairs that led into the Mayfair, where we were about to play our final gig to a sell-out crowd of over two thousand.

I will never forget the reception we got, for as long as I live. From the minute we hit the first note, the crowd went nuts. They were singing along to songs that we had written; those songs meant as much to our audience as they did to us. Nothing has ever come close to the feeling I had on that night. As we left the stage, we could still hear the crowd singing, "Hooray, Hooray."

There have been many great bands who have come out of the North East and many who have gone on to have a great deal more success than we did but on the evening of 26th February 1982, White Heat were the best.

I finally got to bed in the early hours of the morning. My ears were ringing and I was still buzzing from the gig. I kept re-running the previous twenty-four hours over in my head. Eventually, I must have drifted off. I awoke after a couple of hours, with ice in my guts at the realisation that I no longer had a band. Now I really was 'Bob Smeaton who used to be in White Heat'.

My dad. Northumberland All Boys Boxing Champion.

My mam marries the best looking bloke in Benwell.

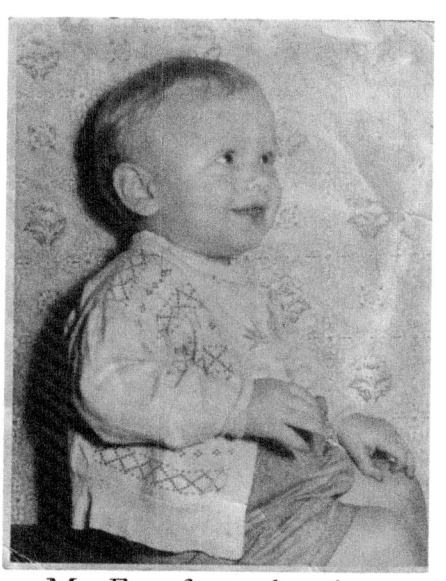

Me. Eyes forward to the future.

Pretending to play Stew Selkirk's Strat left-handed.

(Pic: Stewart Selkirk)

Hartbreaker. Colin Roberts, me in my matching velvet flares and shirt, John Miller, and Bryan Younger with his beard and Les Paul. (Pic: Rik Walton)

Practising the Robert Plant bare-chested look.

Give me half a chance and my shirt would be off.
(Pic: Rik Walton)

White Heat. Alan Fish, Colin Roberts, Bryan Younger, Geordie
Waters and me. The new wave had arrived. (Pic: Rik Walton)

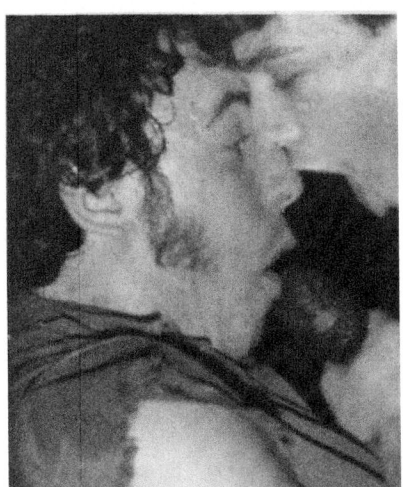

Richard Branson signs my chest backstage at the Venue in London. (Pic: Geordie Waters)

Me and the Boss do a duet at Newcastle City Hall.

White Heat

Virgin Music Publishers Ltd

White Heat at the Marquee Club in London.

FROM THE STAGE TO THE SCREEN

LONDON CALLING

For a couple of weeks after White Heat's final show, I spent time wandering around Newcastle city centre, wallowing in meeting people who told me how great they thought the band were and how it was criminal that we hadn't 'made it'. I was well aware that being in the band had shaped the person that I had become. Any confidence I had came from getting up on stage and performing in front of an audience. Since the day I had quit my job more than two years earlier, White Heat had been my life. Now I had nothing to do and I was desperate to get back to singing in a band; the alternative was too scary to even contemplate.

I didn't see the point in looking to join another Newcastle band. In my opinion, we were the best band in town and anything after White Heat would have been a step-down.

One of things that I had said in the *Check It Out* documentary was that I had made some connections in London which I was hoping to follow up.

I heard through a mutual friend that Chris Pope, the guitarist and songwriter in the Chords - a mod band who had joined us on a couple of the gigs on the Vapours tour - wanted me to get in touch. The Chords had been at the forefront of the recent mod revival and had achieved considerable success. Chris said he had heard that White Heat had split up. He did mention that he thought the band were shit but that I was great, and that the Chords had also recently split and he was in the process of putting together a new band, Agent Orange. He wanted me to be the singer. With this in mind, I travelled to London to meet him.

Chris played me his songs. They were great. He also made it clear that he was the main songwriter in the band and that my role would be purely that of singer and frontman. We did two rehearsals and then were in the studio to record. The sessions were paid for by Polydor Records, the label that the Chords had been signed to. They were going to have first option on this new band.

Mick Talbot, the keyboard player with the Merton Parkers, came along and played on the recording sessions. There was talk that Mick might join the band but instead he became Paul Weller's partner in the Style Council.

When Polydor heard the results of the recordings, they were interested in signing the band but first they wanted to see us perform live.

After the struggles that White Heat had gone through to attract record company attention, this all seemed way too easy, but that was the benefit of being London-based. I knew that I had a decision to make. I didn't want to sign a deal with a label and then drop the lads in it by bailing out. I told Chris that I had come to the conclusion that Agent Orange was not for me. If the truth be told, I hated being away from Newcastle. My return from London was not quite with my tail between my legs but neither was my head held high.

THE COLOUR PROGRAMME

Not long after returning from London, I was in the Portland pub having a drink with Geoff Wonfor. He introduced me to Paul Corley, a producer for BBC TV. Paul was telling Geoff that he had been given the job of putting together an arts show called *The Colour Programme* for the local BBC channel and that he was looking for presenters. Geoff told Paul, "Give Bob the job, he'd be great." TV presenting was not something I had ever considered. Regardless, I chatted with Paul for around half an hour and told him about being in a band and the sort of music I liked. At the end of our chat Paul said, "That all sounds great, Bob, can you start on Monday?" I didn't even have to audition.

I turned up at the BBC studios and told the lady on reception that I was one of the presenters on the new arts show. I was told to sign in and that someone would come down to take me to hair and make-up. While I was having my hair and make-up done, someone brought me a cup of tea. I thought to myself, this is the life. Then Paul Corley turned up and told me that my first interview was to be with a local singer.

Brian Johnson was well-known in the North East for having been the lead singer with the band Geordie. During our interview, he told me that he had just been offered another singing job and that when he received the phone call about auditioning, he was not told the name of the band but he had been given the initials 'ACDC'. It was probably the first time Brian told that story on film but I am sure he has told it a million times since.

One morning, I turned up at the studio and Paul Corley pulled me to one side.

Here we go, I thought, they've probably decided that I am not cut out for the presenting lark. But, surprisingly, Paul told me he thought I was doing a good job, and that he was the one soon to be leaving the BBC. He had been approached by Tyne Tees to produce a music show that was going to go out live on the newly formed Channel Four, on a Friday night. Paul suggested I audition for the role of one of the presenters, thinking that with my background in music and his support I would stand a good chance of getting the job. I thought about it but decided it wasn't for me. I couldn't really see myself as a full-on TV presenter; local telly was fine but I didn't fancy a nationwide programme.

One person who was up for a gig on the new show was my mate Geoff Wonfor. Geoff had shown what he could do as far as directing rock and roll when he had made the *Check It Out* documentary on White Heat, and also the promo films he had made for Lindisfarne; this new show would be right up his street. As expected, Geoff got the gig as one of the principal directors on the new series. The first episode of *The Tube* was broadcast on 5th November 1982. The show ran for five years and revolutionised music television in the UK; it would prove to be a great learning ground for Geoff and he also became big mates with Jools Holland, one of the presenters.

LIFE ON THE FARM

Having finished my tenure as a TV presenter, I got a call from Dave Holly, a theatrical agent based in Newcastle. Dave seemed to represent almost every actor in the North East and was responsible for providing supporting roles and background artists to work on the many TV productions that were happening in our neck of the woods. A large percentage of the people on Dave's books were musicians or comedians who performed on the working men's clubs circuit, who would do 'extra work' to supplement their income. I had never met Dave Holly before but he spoke like he knew me and explained that he was calling to check on my availability to attend a casting for a film about a family who owned a sheep farm on the Scottish borders. The auditions were being held the following Saturday morning at the Station Hotel, next to the railway station in Newcastle. I was to be there at 10.40 a.m.

I went along and met the director, Michael Darlow, and the producer, Tom Sachs. They introduced me to Michael Wilcox, the writer. Michael had written a play called *Accounts*, which had been a big success on the stage. Michael gave me a brief rundown of his play, how it told the story of a Geordie family who own a farm on the borders of Scotland, and the struggles they go through when the father of the family dies and they have to come to terms with running the farm in his absence. The two central characters in the play were brothers Andy and Donald Mawson.

Michael Wilcox told me that he had seen me walking down Northumberland Street in Newcastle, and also presenting the *Colour Programme*, and thought that I had the right sort of attitude to play the part of Andy Mawson. When *Accounts* had been performed on stage the role had been played by Kevin Whatley. Kevin is a brilliant actor who became a household name when he played the role of Detective Sergeant Lewis in the *Inspector Morse* television series. As great as Kevin was in the stage version of the play he would be too old to carry off the character of Andy on screen.

Michael Darlow handed me the script and asked me to read it. As I began, everyone in the room started laughing. I might not have been a great actor but I never expected laughter at my first attempt. Darlow asked me to start again but not to read so fast. When I had finished, he asked me if I had done any acting before. I told him that I had once been in a school play when I was nine, and I had sung in a rock band for eight years. He nodded and said, "Yeah, that figures." He then asked if I had ever spent any time on a farm.

"No," I replied.

"Well, thanks for coming in, Bob, it's been really good to meet you. We will let you know."

By the time Dave Holly rang me a week later and asked me to come down to his office for a chat, I had forgotten about the casting. When I got there, he told me that he was going to be my theatrical agent. I had been offered the part of Andy Mawson in the film and we would start shooting in Kelso in four weeks' time. I couldn't believe it; there must have been hundreds of more experienced actors who were contenders for the role but it turned out that Michael Wilcox had put his neck on the line for me and, even with my lack of acting ability, thought I had the potential to do the job.

Two weeks before filming was due to start, I was sent a copy of the script. I had pretty much learned it off by heart by the time I arrived in Kelso during the spring of 1983. The role of the second brother, Donald, was to be played by a guy called Michael McNally, who had once appeared on *Opportunity Knocks* in his dad's band, Mike Mason and the Little People. Michael was a great bloke and we became fast friends but, just like real-life brothers, we could argue and fight like cat and dog.

Once we began filming, Michael Darlow had to tell me on numerous occasions to stop waving my arms around. "You're not on stage with your rock band now, you're not playing to the back of the room. Make all your gestures smaller, and stop trying to act." I think I knew what he meant and eventually I started to get the hang of it.

I decided that that when the film was released I would be credited as Robert Smeaton rather than Bob. My thinking was that I was moving on from being 'Bob Smeaton that used to be in White Heat'. I hoped I would be joining a long line of Roberts, such as De Niro and Redford. When I travelled to London for a press screening of the film I was disappointed when my name appeared on the credits and wished that I had stuck to Bob Smeaton.

Three months after we 'wrapped', *Accounts* was shown on television. I wondered if the careers guidance lady I met nine years earlier was watching. Maybe next time she had some slightly nervous young bloke sat in front of her with big ideas about being a singer or an actor, she might think twice before handing them an application form for the shipyards.

YOU CAN TAKE THE BOY OUT OF NEWCASTLE

Having had such a great time making *Accounts*, I began to think I might give this acting lark a go. I went to see Dave and told him to start putting me up for stuff. I attended loads of auditions. Unlike when I had attended the casting for *Accounts*, I never got any calls that told me I had got the part. I was often asked the same question when I went to castings: "Can you try reading it without your accent?"

Eventually, the penny began to drop. If I was going to pursue my career as an actor, I was going to have to learn to speak without my Geordie accent.

I did some research and learned that the best person to see with regards to learning how to speak without an accent was a woman called Joan Washington. I called Joan, told her what I wanted to do and asked her if she was up for the challenge. She told me to come down to Richmond on the outskirts of London and we would have a chat about it. I went along and met her and she was convinced that after about ten lessons, as long as I did my homework, she could have me speaking without my accent as and when it suited me.

We would sit at her dining table, read passages from a book, and work on my vowel sounds. It was like being back in school but Joan was a great teacher and remained patient with me, giving me a load of encouragement when I felt like giving up. After a couple of months, I thought I was sounding pretty good.

In a cab to King's Cross, I thought I would try out my new non-Geordie accent on the cab driver. "Can you take me to King's Cross, please?" In my head, I sounded like Hugh Grant.

"Yeah, no problem, mate," he replied.

For the rest of the journey, I was chatting away with him and thinking to myself, I've got this bloke fooled. I was even contemplating dropping in a bit of the old cockney rhyming slang but I didn't want to push my luck. Just before we arrived at King's Cross, the conversation turned to football and he asked me, "Who's your team then, guv'nor, Sunderland?"

Bloody hell, these lessons were costing me fifty quid a pop and I was sounding like a Makem (a person from Sunderland). Not wanting to feel too downhearted, I tried out my accent on the people I met on the train but the further north I got, the more northern my accent became. By the time we had crossed the Tyne Bridge, I sounded more James Bolam than James Mason.

I wasn't going to give up, though, and would learn my audition piece for casting agents in my new posh accent, only to be told at the end of a read, "That was really good, Bob, now can you try it without your Geordie accent." There were even times when I was asked if I was Welsh, and once got asked what part of Ireland I came from. It seemed like you could take the boy out of Newcastle but you couldn't take the Geordie accent out of the boy. In fact, the next job I got - after spending a fortune on voice coaching and train fairs to London - was a voice-over for the *Daily Star* newspaper. I was required to say in my best Geordie accent, "The *Daily Star*, it's a right rivetin' read."

Needless to say, I wasn't going to be taking any jobs from Rupert Everett.

But I did land a role in the Catherine Cookson drama *The Black Candle*. Every Geordie actor who was a member of Equity (the actors' union) would eventually end up with a part in 'A Cookson'. I was cast in a supporting role, playing Fred Skinner; a dodgy character who tries to bribe some rich bloke played by the actor Nathaniel Parker. In the film, I had to have a fight with Nathaniel. While we were rehearsing the scene, the director had to point out to me that it was not a real fight and that we were meant to be acting. It is after my fight scene, which occurs about fifteen minutes into the film, that I end up getting my throat cut. I should have known those posh blokes would fight dirty. And that was the end of Fred Skinner.

My mam says my role in *The Black Candle* is still the best thing that I have ever done. It gets repeated a lot on Tyne Tees and it would appear that she never grows tired of seeing me get my throat cut. She must have watched it around twenty times. Now she is able to watch it any time she pleases as a couple of years ago the DVD of the film was given away free with her Sunday paper. Despite having the DVD, she still watches it whenever it is on the telly. She knows the script off by heart. Often now when I go to visit her she says, "Shall we watch *The Black Candle*?" Before I have a chance to protest, it's in the DVD player.

The conversation while we watch it often goes along these lines: "It's funny, isn't it, son, that on the telly we have just watched you get your throat cut, but here you are still alive." She then goes on to tell me that I should have been able to 'chin' that posh bloke. I have to point out to her, just as it was pointed out to me by the director, that I was acting and it was not real life.

THE ONE YOU'VE GOT TO COME BACK FOR

When Dave put me up for a role in a beer commercial, I had no idea that it would give me a glimpse of what it was like to be famous and to be recognised on the street. I arrived in London to audition for the ad to discover that I was there along with about twenty other blokes. I was called into the room to meet the casting director and the people from the ad agency; well, to say I met them was an overstatement. I was told to say my name and the name of my agent to camera. I did this, and then the casting director said, "Thanks very much, we will let you know." I must have been in that room for two minutes, then I was on the train back to Newcastle. What a waste of time and money.

When I got back to my flat, the phone was ringing. It was Dave, calling to tell me I had the job. The advert was being filmed one week later; the exteriors were going to be filmed in Newcastle and the interior shots would be on a set in London.

The night before the Newcastle shoot, I was invited to the Fisherman's Warf, 'Newcastle's number one seafood restaurant', to meet the production team. When I arrived, I was pointed in the direction of a table that was set out like a banquet. It was adorned with a whole family of lobsters and a host of ice buckets that were being used to keep the champagne chilled. Around the table sat the production team, who had just arrived up from London and must have been feeling really hungry and thirsty after their three-hour train journey!

I was introduced to the director, David Mallet, who told me the idea for the advert. The theme was based around a guy from Newcastle who leaves his home town and his girlfriend, to seek his fame and fortune in London. He returns after a year or so to discover that his girlfriend has got engaged to some other bloke but he's not bothered because what he was really returning home for was a pint of his favourite beer, McEwan's Best Scotch.

At the time, Paul Young was riding high in the singles chart with his cover of the Marvin Gaye classic, *Wherever I Lay My Hat (That's My Home)*. In the advert, the line was changed to 'It's only when I see McEwan's Scotch I know I'm home'. Genius!!

David also explained to me that to appear in a beer commercial, not only did you have to be over twenty-seven years of age but you had to look it. The people at the agency thought I looked younger than that. David decided the best way to make me look older was to get me steaming drunk so that I would turn up the next day looking knackered. It worked; I turned up for filming with a stinking hangover and looking like shit.

A couple of days after filming in Newcastle, we shot the rest of the ad in what was meant to be the inside of a pub, on a set in London. There I was, in what was meant to be my home-town pub, which was filled with a load of extras who were meant to be my mates. As I was chatting to them, I discovered that none of them had ever been north of Watford. That's the magic of television.

At the end of the final day of filming, I was told that the ad would be airing the following Thursday night, at 7.30. I sat in my flat and watched it go out for the first time. It looked great and I was well pleased with myself. Thanks to YouTube, you can now view the advert online.

The Friday night following the first time the advert had aired, I headed down to the Bigg Market in Newcastle for a drink with my mates. It was a nightmare.

Total strangers would approach me. "Are you that bloke off the McEwan's Scotch advert?"

"Yes," I would reply.

"Well, you're a wanker."

If girls spoke to me and asked me the same question, more often than not they would be with their boyfriends, who would want to punch me for, as they saw it, thinking that just because I was on the telly I could chat up their girlfriends. The bouncers on the doors to the pubs would say to each other as I walked in to keep an eye out because somebody was bound to punch me.

Catching the bus back to my flat in Benwell on a Friday night was scary at the best of times but when you were 'that wanker off that advert' it was even worse. No sooner would I be in my seat than I would feel the tap on my shoulder and some bloke would want to have a go at me. I got involved in so many fights it was ridiculous, and if I got a pound for every time I was asked the question, "Are you that wanker from the McEwan's Best Scotch advert?" I would be a very rich man.

One person who was now on his way to becoming a very rich man and had never - to my knowledge - appeared in a beer commercial was the guitarist Andy Taylor. Andy had once shared a flat with an ex-girlfriend of mine and would often come along to see White Heat. One morning, Andy headed off to Birmingham to audition for a band that had management and were looking for a guitarist. He got the job and in the summer of 1983 he and the other guys in Duran Duran were flying high in the charts.

As a sideline to his day job, Andy and a couple of his bandmates opened a bar called Rio's, down near the sea front in Whitley Bay. Andy got in touch and invited me to the opening. When I arrived outside the bar it was like Beatlemania. As I was walking in, some girls recognised me and started screaming, "Hey look, there's that bloke off the McEwan's Scotch advert."

My heart sank. I had appeared in a thirty-second beer commercial and was getting more recognition for that than for being in a band for eight years. It all seemed wrong. I was no longer 'Bob Smeaton who used to be in White Heat' but 'that bloke off the McEwan's advert'.

But there was an upside.

BOB AND RACHEL

One of the perks of being a 'local celebrity' was that I would often be invited to be a judge at many of the beauty contests that were held in a number of the bars in town. This was back in 1984 when hosting a beauty contest was an accepted way of getting blokes into bars, to look at good looking girls walking around in bikinis. Despite my embarrassment, I was afforded the best seat in the house and given free drinks for the duration of the evening. On one occasion, I was judging at a bar called Legends but rather than look at the girls who had entered the competition, my eye was caught by another girl, on the other side of the bar.

As I left, the same girl was waiting outside. I went up and started talking to her. She told me that her name was Rachel and that she had come along to support her sister Ruth, who had entered the competition. Rachel looked even better close up than she had from ten feet away. She really was the best looking girl that I had ever seen on Tyneside. As it turned out, I wasn't the only person who thought this. In fact, she was the best looking girl on Tyneside *and* Wearside, as was proven six months after we started dating when she herself entered a beauty contest and was crowned Miss Tyne and Wear.

Rachel and I moved into a flat together above a hairdressing salon on the corner of Kenton Road. It was great. I had an endless supply of hair products and would even take to sitting under the hairdryers when I was in a hurry to get ready for a night out, of which there were many. We were like Newcastle's answer to Mick and Bianca Jagger. We would be invited along to any new pub or nightclub that was opening in Newcastle. We also became good friends with Joe Robinson, the man who was dubbed Mr Newcastle, based upon the fact that he was credited with revolutionising the drinking habits in the North East. Joe had opened a string of bars in the Bigg Market and on the Quayside. He was the first person I ever saw carrying a mobile phone and he drove a white Rolls Royce with the registration number 'JOE 90'.

We got invited onto Joe's boat in the South of France and I would often get to watch Newcastle play from the comfort of his executive box at St James' Park. I had come a long way from standing on the terraces: here I was, sat in a comfortable chair while waitresses served me champagne and brought me sandwiches.

On the surface, it would look like everything was going great. I was dating the best looking girl in Newcastle and hanging out on yachts in the South of France. But if the truth be told, my acting career was hardly going in leaps and bounds and any money that I had earned from doing the advert had long gone. In fact, for my next acting job not only did I not have to speak any lines, I didn't even appear on screen.

Dave Holly rang and asked, "Bob can you work a puppet?" "What do you mean, Dave?" I replied, "Have you put me up for a job in a Punch and Judy show?" As it turned out he had put me forward for a new series that was being made by the Jim Henson Organisation, the same people who had made *The Muppet Show*. The show was going to be called *The Ghost of Faffner Hall*. I went along to the studio at Tyne Tees where the series was going to be made and where the auditions were being held.

I arrived and met Richard Hunt, the voice of Fozzie Bear. Richard handed me a mouse puppet that was about two foot tall and told me to invent a character for the mouse. I slid my arm inside and with my hand in its head I started moving the mouth and talking in a high-pitched Geordie accent. Richard thought this was hilarious and told me he didn't have a clue what 'Max the Mouse' was saying but that it sounded really funny. He also mentioned that being left-handed would work to my advantage as left-handed puppeteers were in short supply.

I got the job and spent a very happy couple of months working with the Henson people. But sadly Max the Mouse never scaled the dizzy heights of Kermit the frog and basically remained a background artist. My fortunes after finishing on *The Ghost of Faffner Hall* seemed to be mirroring that of Max and the only work I was offered was also as a background artist.

Eventually, I had to sign on the dole. Each week, I would turn up at the dole office and more often than not the person behind the counter would have seen me on the telly or when I was in the band and would ask me what I was up to now. It was demoralising and I hated it, but I was skint and that thirty quid a week was a life-saver, but it didn't go very far when I was hanging out at Julie's nightclub on the Quayside three times a week.

In order to supplement my dole money, I bit the bullet and auditioned for a 'club band' who I was told needed a singer. I got the gig and we began rehearsing a set of cover versions that included *Every Breath You Take* by the Police and *True* by Spandau Ballet. I didn't mind the Police song but I hated *True*.

Martin Campbell, the guitarist in the band, was a really good looking guy from Bedlington. He was like a long-haired version of John Travolta. Hearing him play guitar was the high point of the rehearsals. The lowest point was when one of the band suggested we cover Paul Young's version of *Wherever I Lay My Hat*. He thought it would be a great idea to have the bloke off the ad sing the song, he said it would bring the house down. I thought, 'yeah, and my reputation with it'. I couldn't believe that I had gone from playing Newcastle City Hall and selling out the Mayfair to being faced with the prospect of appearing second on the bill to the bingo at a working man's club.

As it happened, fate intervened. The day before we were due to play our first gig, the drummer got sick and the gig was cancelled. I never got to do my very bad impersonation of Tony Hadley.

FAMOUS FOR FIFTEEN MINUTES

On the wall of my flat I had pinned a picture of Sting that I had cut from an article which had run in *Rolling Stone* magazine. Sting was a bit of a hero of mine and a big inspiration, having made the giant leap from being the son of a milkman in Wallsend to become one of the biggest rock stars in the world. In the photograph, Sting was wearing a white string vest and looked fit, suntanned, super cool, and as handsome as all hell. I read in the interview that Sting had kept a diary from when he was a kid up to the present day. I decided to do the same and have kept a diary ever since. Reading those diaries now, I realise how desperate I was becoming, but also how determined I was to succeed. I had an acute fear of having nothing to do and dreaded bumping into anyone who knew me and being asked, "What are you up to, Bob?" Aside from notes about my general state of mind, I would write down how many calories I had consumed that week, how many runs I had been on and how far they were, and the number of times I had been to the gym. I knew I had to keep myself in shape for when 'my time came' and I always felt that time was just around the corner. I used to have nightmares in which I would end up back in the shipyards, and I would be explaining to my old workmates that I was only back temporarily. I would wake up in a cold sweat.

I had remained in regular contact with Geoff Wonfor and one night during the early part of 1987 he told me that Tyne Tees were no longer going to be making *The Tube* and that he and Andy Mathews, who had edited most of the material that Geoff had directed, were going to be leaving and setting up their own television production company called Strictly the Business.

Geoff pitched an idea to Channel Four television for a series that would showcase unsigned bands, on the grounds that it would help fill the gap left by *The Tube*. Channel Four loved the idea and Strictly the Business got their first commission.

Geoff told me, "Bob, you have got to reform White Heat and appear on the show." He was convinced that this would give the band the nationwide exposure that we had never enjoyed before. At first I was reluctant but Geoff talked me into it. If the truth be told, I didn't take that much persuading.

The idea initially was to reform White Heat but under a new name. The only one who wasn't into the idea was guitarist Bryan Younger. I was gutted that Bryan didn't want to be involved; he and I had been instrumental in the band from its formative days over ten years ago and he deserved to share our moment in the spotlight, but I had to respect his decision. Still, we needed that second guitar player. I approached Martin Campbell who I had met when I nearly joined the club band and he jumped at the chance.

I was now hanging out at the Strictly the Business offices every day and was constantly badgering Geoff as to when we could get started on the series. Before we could get moving, however, Geoff had been brought on board to direct a documentary about the story of Island Records and was due to go off to Jamaica to start filming with Chris Blackwell, the record company's founder. One day I was sitting in the office and Geoff said, "Get your passport, you're coming to Jamaica." He had decided he was going to take me to Jamaica in the role of director's assistant but also with a view to possibly shooting some material that we might use in the *Famous for Fifteen Minutes* series.

On 21st May 1987, I landed in Jamaica. I couldn't believe that Geoff had pulled it off. Paul Gambaccini, the American DJ who worked for BBC radio, had also travelled to Jamaica with us, in the capacity of interviewer. I was able to sit in and listen as 'Gambo' chatted to Chris Blackwell, who recounted the story of Island Records.

Geoff shot a number of sequences at Goldeneye, the house that had once been owned by James Bond creator Ian Fleming and which Blackwell had subsequently bought. At the end of one of the shoot days, Geoff was true to his word with regards to filming something for *Famous for Fifteen Minutes*, and shot a video of me lip-syncing to *The Party's Over*, a song that featured the title of the series among its lyrics.

I had to pinch myself. Here I was, making a video in Jamaica, while a week earlier I had been signing on the dole in Newcastle. I was so pleased with myself that I decided to send my dad a postcard, to tell him that I was in Montego Bay and that I remembered this was the title of one of the records he had in his collection when I was growing up. I later found out that he got really pissed off when he received the card; it turned out his new girlfriend had read it and asked who Bob was. He hadn't let on that he had a son my age. He got around the problem by telling his girlfriend that I was not his son but in fact the son of his brother Jimmy, who had recently died, and that since Jimmy's death I had gone a bit mad and had taken to calling him Dad. That was the last postcard I ever sent him.

When we returned from Jamaica and Geoff had finished his Island Records documentary, we started filming the *Fifteen Minutes* series. We shot a live sequence of the band performing in the Riverside Club, where we played a mixture of White Heat songs and a couple of our new songs. I had also written a script for a short drama sequence as an introductory piece to the opening of our programme and had cast myself in the lead role. I thought if the record companies could see that I could act as well as sing, it would be a no-brainer that they would want to sign us.

The next decision to be made was what we were going to call the band. It was me that had done most of the running to get this thing off the ground and I was the one who had spent hours in the edit suite with Andy Matthews and Geoff Wonfor. I was very aware that this could well be my last throw of the dice. At nine p.m. on Friday 30th October, the first band to appear on Channel Four's new series *Famous for Fifteen Minutes* was Bob Smeaton and the Loud Guitars.

AN OFFER YOU COULDN'T REFUSE

After one gig, I was approached by a guy who introduced himself as Ronnie Fowler, who asked me if I had a record deal and handed me his business card. As it turned out, Ronnie was working for Jet Records, who had been responsible for signing ELO and Ozzy Osbourne. Ronnie suggested I come to London the following week and meet 'the boss' at his office in Wimbledon.

I sat in reception and looked at the gold records that adorned the walls. Eventually, I was told, "OK, you can go in now." I walked into the office and there, sat behind a leather desk with gold studs running down the sides, was a bloke who looked more like a gangster than a record company boss. In fact, he had a distinct look of Al Capone about him. I was sat on a little chair looking up at him and he rose out of his seat, shook my hand and said, "Pleased to meet you, Bob, you can call me Don." I already had a feeling he was going to make me an offer I couldn't refuse.

"Ronnie tells me you're a great singer and frontman and that you don't have a record deal at the minute, is that true?"

"Yes," I replied. I wasn't sure whether or not to call him sir.

"OK, son, well I would like to sign you to my label, and put you on the road in America, that's the way to make it."

It was like a dream and I felt like I needed to use the toilet; I wasn't sure if it was with fear or excitement. Then Don said, "But first things first, who do we have to get rid of?"

I nearly shit myself. "What do you mean, Don, who do we have to get rid of?"

Don explained to me that before he got involved in any contract discussions he would need to know who was going to start coming out of the woodwork and start claiming that they owned a piece of me. I explained that Laurie Dunn had signed me to Virgin Music but I had originally signed a deal with Brian Mawson, my former manager. I handed over Brian's and Laurie's phone numbers.

"OK, Bob, leave it with me."

I stood up to leave and my legs were shaking. I had just met Don Arden.

When I got back to Newcastle, I went to see Brian to tell him to expect a call from Don Arden. He went white. It transpired that Don Arden had a fearsome reputation within the music business. Legend has it that he had once dangled a record company executive out of a fourth-floor office window. He had also managed the Small Faces, who by all accounts had broken up skint. Don Arden was the father of Sharon Arden, who later married Ozzy Osbourne. I hadn't been aware of any of this at the time that I had travelled down to meet him. But the promise of touring America sounded too good to pass up and hey, nobody's perfect.

A couple of days later, Brian got in touch and explained that someone had called him on behalf of Don Arden to say that he was now going to be 'looking after me'. It turned out that someone had also been in touch with Laurie Dunn and told him the same thing. Laurie rang to tell me that if I wanted to sign with Don Arden he wouldn't stand in my way but to be careful and get advice before I entered into any contractual discussions.

A week or so later, Ronnie Fowler got in touch with me and told me that my contractual situation was in a mess, that Brian Mawson said he owned my music publishing and the guy at Virgin Music had said that they owned the rights. Ronnie went on to say that Don had decided that to try and free me from that mess was going to be more bother than it was worth. I never heard from Don Arden again.

THE PARTY'S OVER

The exposure we gained from appearing on *Famous for Fifteen Minutes* was not the springboard I had hoped it would be. There was a smattering of interest from a number of record companies but the offers of a contract never transpired. Regardless, we decided to continue doing gigs in and around Newcastle.

We eventually dropped the 'Bob Smeaton' and just went out as the Loud Guitars. Pretty soon we'd built up a sizeable following. We had a bunch of good songs and the lads in the band were all great musicians. The role of drummer would change constantly and at varying times the drum stool was filled by, among others, Brian Dick (who had been in local heavy metal band the Tygers of Pan Tang), Stu Haikney, and John Trotter. We also added a keyboard player, Gary Cowey, and enlisted another former Tyger of Pan Tang when Dave Donaldson joined the band on backing vocals.

We even went as far as releasing an independent single called *A Different Man* and Geoff was going to direct a video for it. We had an idea that all the band would appear as if we were characters in an American TV series. I cast myself in the role of a toilet cleaner; this was a veiled dig at my dad, who had said I would never amount to anything. Well, he was right. Here I was cleaning toilets. I was also captioned as 'Bob Smeaton JNR'. My thinking behind this was that if my dad and his new girlfriend happened to see the video, there would be questions asked about this other Bob Smeaton, seeing as my dad's brother was called Jimmy.

The record sold really well and we found ourselves at the top of the North East charts but there was a feeling that we had been here before. Also, if the truth be told, it would appear that the desire to rise above being a 'local band' was no longer there and, for some members, being in a band was not the most important thing in life any longer. We were all older than when we were chasing the dream with White Heat. Wives, mortgages and families had entered the equation. In fact, I was the only member of the band that was not married. Rachel and I had got engaged a couple of years earlier but now, after seven years together, we had begun to drift apart. She was a great girl and stood by me through all my various ups and downs, and if the truth be told I had probably neglected her while I was busy focusing on the band and my obsession with making it. Not long after we broke up, she started dating a doctor. They subsequently married and started a family.

I knew that the Loud Guitars calling it a day was going to leave a massive void in my life. I was now thirty-three and pretty much resigned to the fact that I was not going to make it as a rock star. Being a singer in a band was the greatest thing that I had ever done, and nothing would ever replace that feeling of being on stage. The Loud Guitars used to perform the Animals' song *Good Times*. The lyrics of the song about the good time that we waste having good times always resonated with me. But, as I was soon to find out, the fifteen years I had spent having good times as a singer in a band had not been wasted.

ALL YOU NEED IS GEOFF

For the next ten years there was barely a day that went by when Geoff Wonfor and I didn't spend time in each other's company. Geoff was able to wangle me onto any job that he was working on; I think initially he got me involved because he liked having me around.

I learned so much from watching Geoff work. He would say to the crew, "OK, everybody happy, turn over." The cameras would roll and off we would go. He had such a positive attitude, everyone that worked with him loved him. He could also tell a great story and whenever we were on a shoot he would regale us with his stories of his days filming *The Tube*. I spent so much time hanging around with Geoff that I knew his stories off by heart. But I would still listen intently, laugh and nod encouragement.

Geoff would often ask me, "How are you for money?" Before I would have a chance to answer, he would stick fifty quid in my hand and tell me, "Here, take this, pay me it back when you've got some money." When I tried to repay him weeks later, he wouldn't take it and would tell me to buy myself something. He also liked a bet on the horses and whenever he won he would bung me twenty quid or a share of his winnings. Often, when he was losing again, he would ask for the money back as a loan. I soon learnt to spend whatever he had given me.

If Geoff was asked to make a promotional video for a band that he had never heard of he would ask me who they were and if they were any good. One such band was the Stone Roses. I told Geoff they were a band from Manchester who were being tipped in the music press as the 'next big thing'. Geoff spoke to the management of the band and was told that they had got in touch with him because they 'didn't want to use any London wankers' and wanted to use someone from the north. Us northerners like to stick together. We ended up shooting the videos for *She Bangs the Drums* and *Fools Gold*.

After *The Tube*, Geoff and Jools Holland continued working together. During the summer of 1990, they were heading off to Memphis and Nashville to make a film that was going to be called *Mr Roadrunner*. England had just been knocked out of the World Cup so when Geoff told me he was taking me with him in the role of director's assistant, it was just what I needed to raise my spirits.

One of the first sequences that we filmed in Memphis was Jools chatting to Charlie Rich. Charlie was probably best known for his hit singles *Behind Closed Doors* and *The Most Beautiful Girl in the World*. He was also one of the first artists signed to Sam Philips' Sun Records, home to the likes of Elvis Presley and Roy Orbison. When Charlie turned up for the shoot he must have been thinking, 'Here we go again, another bunch of British guys who don't know their rock and roll history.' Judging by his demeanour it looked like he wanted to get in, do the interview, and get out of there as quickly as possible.

Jools sat next to Charlie at the piano and began to play *Lonely Weekends,* a song that he had recorded for Sam Philips in 1960. As soon as Jools started playing, Charlie's attitude changed. He knew he was in the company of a fellow musician and someone who really knew their stuff.

Jools is not only a great musician. I never once saw him lose his temper or his patience and for him being on the shoot was as much about having a good time as getting the job done.

Another musician who had been lined up for us to film was rhythm and blues legend Rufus Thomas. We travelled out to a town on the outskirts of Memphis to film him in a tiny club. When we arrived, Rufus told us this was the sort of place where they ask you at the door if you have a gun and, if you don't, they give you one. We hoped he was joking.

When we got into the club we were the only white faces in the place but the atmosphere was fantastic; we couldn't have been made more welcome. Everyone was there for one thing and one thing only, and that was to see Rufus Thomas. The idea was that Rufus would play a live set of his songs and then in the middle, specifically for the benefit of the film crew, he would mime to his big hit *Walking the Dog*.

At the chosen moment, our sound guy hit the button for *Walking the Dog*. When the audience heard the opening to the song, the whole place went crazy. Guys were dragging girls onto the dance floor and were 'walking the dog'. About a quarter of the way into the song, Rufus started waving his arms around and telling the sound guy to stop the playback. In front of the packed club, Rufus gave his guitarist a bollocking and told him he was playing the wrong notes. The guitarist wasn't even plugged into his amp but Rufus knew the song so well that when he looked at the guitar player during the solo he could see that he was not miming the right notes. I guess when you've performed a song thousands of times you get to know where the guitarist's fingers are meant to be. That's why Rufus Thomas is a legend. They ran the playback again and this time the guitarist made sure that he was miming the right notes.

At the end of the trip, we had a day off before returning home. Any visit to Tennessee would not have been complete without a trip to Graceland, the former home of The King. The chance to visit Graceland was too good to pass up. We were not allowed to go upstairs in Elvis' house but were shown around the place. I must admit I was a bit disappointed with his taste in decoration. One room was decorated like a jungle; one thing is for sure, Elvis didn't do his furniture shopping at IKEA.

I decided to take a walk over to the spot in the grounds where Elvis was buried. It was a very solemn moment as I stood next to the grave. I handed my camera to one of the guys in our crew and asked if he would take a picture of me next to Elvis' final resting place. The guy I handed the camera to seemed to find the whole thing hilarious, in fact the whole of the crew seemed to find it hilarious that I would want my picture taken next to a grave. It was only when I got back to Newcastle and got my pictures developed that I realised I had in fact been standing next to the grave of Elvis' twin brother Jesse, who had died at birth. No one on the crew thought to point this out to me at the time.

A couple of weeks after filming in America with legends such as Charlie Rich and Rufus Thomas, we were back in Newcastle and filming with a different kind of legend: Paul Gascoigne. Following England's defeat in the World Cup, Paul Gascoigne had become a national hero, after being sent off during the semi-final against West Germany. Gazza's emotional response to his red card had endeared him to the nation. Some bright spark in his camp thought it would be a good idea for him to record a song, to capitalise on his new-found fame. The song that he decided to record to celebrate his standing as a national treasure was the old Lindisfarne classic, *Fog on the Tyne*. Now, what this song has got to do with being sent off in the World Cup was beyond me, but he was a local lad and Lindisfarne were a local band so I guess there was some method in the madness.

We shot a video of Gazza travelling up the River Tyne on a boat as he gave his stirring rendition of the Lindisfarne classic. We also filmed in a local club and he appeared on stage, backed by the guys from Lindisfarne. There were a lot of words in that song and Gazza hadn't learnt them so part of my job was to hold up dummy boards so that he could sing along. In amongst the crowd were a couple of followers of White Heat. I remembered them looking at me as if to say, 'Bob, has it come to this?'

The record stormed up the charts to number two. How much this had to do with the video, I have no idea. Geoff also filmed the video for Gazza's follow-up single, *Geordie Boys*. I think I was sick on the day they filmed that one.

The nature of the job was that one week we could be filming Gazza on a boat floating up the Tyne and the next we could be in Liverpool

Cathedral, filming Paul McCartney's *Liverpool Oratorio*. One day, during a break in filming, Geoff said to me, "Come on, Bob, I'm going to take you to meet Macca." I walked into the canteen and there was Paul McCartney. He looked great and the strange thing was, he looked just like Paul McCartney. Geoff sat chatting to Paul who, for being one of the biggest pop stars on the planet, seemed like a really down-to-earth bloke.

During a break in the conversation, I decided to asked Paul what it was like when he met Elvis. I had never spoken to anyone who had met the King before and knew this was my chance. Paul said that the Beatles had met Elvis when they were in Los Angeles in 1965. I asked Paul if it was true that John Lennon, upon meeting Elvis, had turned to him and said, "Where's Elvis?" Paul said he wasn't sure that they were John's exact words but it sounded like the sort of thing that John would have said. He then got up and went off to continue rehearsing with the orchestra. Once he had left the table, Geoff turned to me and said, "I cannot believe it. You meet Paul McCartney, the most famous musician in the world, and you ask him a question about Elvis Presley and then follow that up with a question about John Lennon." But Geoff didn't stay pissed off with me for very long; in fact, I think he found it funny that I had the audacity to ask those questions.

I knew for certain that he wasn't pissed off when he mentioned that he had a big gig coming up that he wanted to get me involved in. He couldn't say what it was at present but it was going to be the biggest gig in the world.

THE LONG AND WINDING ROAD

THE BIGGEST GIG IN THE WORLD

I was stood in Newcastle Central train station on a freezing-cold December morning. The previous day, Geoff Wonfor had asked me to pick him up as he was getting the early train back from London King's Cross. As I suspected, Geoff was not on the train that he said he was going to be on and if he'd had a bit of a night out in London there was no guarantee he was even going to be on the next one.

When the next train arrived, I looked through the crowd to see if I could spot him but I heard him before I saw him. He was singing at the top of his voice and he might have even been doing a little dance. 'Fucking hell,' I thought to myself, 'he's still drunk.'

As Geoff got closer to me, I realised that he wasn't drunk; he was just the happiest that I had ever seen him.

"It's on," Geoff said to me.

"What's on?"

"The gig, the one I couldn't tell you about, it's happening. We are starting in January next year, it's the biggest gig in rock and roll, it's all agreed, the contracts are signed, and you and Andy Mathews are both on board."

When Geoff told me what it was, it was the best Christmas present I had ever had. He wasn't exaggerating, it *was* the biggest gig in rock and roll. We were going to be making a documentary on the most famous band in the world, the Beatles.

On the morning of 14th January 1992, Geoff, Andy Mathews and I drove to London to have a meeting with a guy called Neil Aspinall, to discuss a plan and a schedule for the making of a documentary that would tell the Beatles story. Neil Aspinall had been the Beatles' road manager back in the days before they became the biggest band in the world and now he was running Apple Corps, the company the Beatles had set up in the late 1960s.

Neil was a friendly Liverpudlian who still spoke with his Scouse accent; in fact, if you closed your eyes you could have been talking to John Lennon. Neil might have been friendly but I immediately got the impression that he wouldn't take shit from anyone. After the Beatles broke up, Neil had continued working for them and one of the things he had been doing since the mid-1970s was pulling together archive footage, with a view to one day making a documentary. Neil showed us a cut of what he had assembled and the archive looked great but there wasn't any narrative; none of the Beatles were included in interview. Neil had originally given the project the working title of *The Long and Winding Road*. When we arrived at the offices of Apple, the project was now going under the working title of *The History of the Beatles*.

Neil was a big fan of a Ken Burns documentary series that told the story of the American Civil War. When that had been broadcast in America during 1990, the ten-hour documentary had reached an audience of over 50 million. Neil thought that the Beatles were worthy of a documentary of that size and scope. The idea that Neil had was that *The History of the Beatles* would be released as a series of VHS tapes (this was back in 1992 and DVD was yet to be invented). Neil stipulated that if the Beatles were not happy with what we were making, it would never see the light of day.

He also said he wanted every Beatles single release to run full-length in the documentary. His other stipulation was that he didn't want to use voice-over. It had to be their story in their own words. The only people who would be interviewed would be the group themselves, and possibly George Martin, their record producer. We suggested that Neil should also be interviewed and he said, "Well, let's wait and see about that." But I think he quite liked the idea.

The Beatles could have enlisted the services of any film-maker they wanted to bring Neil's idea to fruition. There had been talk that Steven Spielberg had been in the frame, along with George Lucas, but, like anything the Beatles did, they all had to agree upon it. Geoff had worked with McCartney on the *Liverpool Oratorio* and George Harrison had featured in the *Mr Roadrunner* documentary. Geoff had also done a piece on Ringo for *The Tube* so he was a known entity.

Initially, Neil was going to produce the series but Geoff pointed out that he would be too tied up dealing with the day-to-day running of Apple. Geoff suggested that Chips Chipperfield, who was running the television and video wing of EMI, be brought on board to produce, and that Neil take on the role of executive producer. Chips was another northerner and he and I would become really close during the making of the series.

Originally, we had thought that the whole process would take a year to eighteen months at the most. Neil said, "It will take as long as it takes."

For the first couple of months, I never let on to any of my friends back in Newcastle that I was working on a Beatles project. This was like a dream come true but I wasn't counting my chickens. I was worried that any day soon I was going to be told, "Sorry, Bob, we don't need you, you are surplus to requirements." My job title at the time was Director's Assistant. I wasn't even sure what that entailed but whatever it was, I still had the feeling that I was there because Geoff liked having me around. I asked him what my role was and he replied, "You can make it whatever you want it to be, your job is to make me look good."

I took Geoff at his word and decided that I was not going to let this chance pass me by; I was going to make sure I was as close to indispensable as possible. I gave myself an intensive crash course in all things Beatles. I read everything that there was to read about them in order to make sure that I knew their story inside out. I started with *The Complete Beatles Chronicles*, a book by Mark Lewisohn which gave a day-to-day account of everything the Beatles were doing, from the day they formed until they were a band no longer. And if there was anything I was unsure of, I could always pick up the phone and speak to Mark, who had an encyclopaedic knowledge of the Beatles.

I was given all the albums on CD and memorised every song and the running order of each of the albums. I learnt who wrote which songs, and when and where they were written. After three months, I was the in-house expert and if anyone asked a Beatles-related question I knew the answer. I also began to appreciate how great they were. They had written some of the greatest songs of all time, they were much more than 'just another band'. The Beatles had changed the world.

Neil's original idea was that we begin telling the Beatles story from the release of their first single, *Love Me Do*. Geoff, Andy and I were discussing this and I suggested we start right at the beginning, on the day that Ringo was born. This had never been done in a music documentary before; in the few that had been made on the likes of Elvis and the Rolling Stones, the story normally started when they formed the band or when they started getting into music. We all agreed that this was a great idea and that's what we did. The story of the Beatles would be told from 7th July 1940, the day that Richard Starkey was born.

Geoff had suggested that Jools Holland do the interviews with the Beatles, rather than a hardnosed music journalist. I would provide Jools with a set of questions for which we needed the answers in order to tell the Beatles story. If Jools missed anything, it would be my job to jump in at the end of the interview and request that Jools ask something that had been missed.

We had planned to interview the Beatles in fantastic locations such as on the top of mountains, or the Empire State Building; locations that were in scale as big as the Beatles themselves. In the end, Neil decided that what they were going to say was more important than where they were saying it, so that idea went out of the window.

The first interview we did was with Ringo on 6th April. We filmed him at the edit suite that had been installed in some offices that Apple had leased on Wendell Road in Shepherd's Bush. When Ringo came into the room the first thing he said was, "Before anyone asks, I'm not signing any autographs." He seemed a little bit grumpy and not the loveable, wisecracking Beatle that I had been watching on archive for the past four months.

We hadn't really got off to a great start but Ringo soon began to get into it and once he realised that we were on his side he was great. When he was telling us about his childhood days in Liverpool, I knew that we had made the right decision to go back to the beginning, when he was just another kid growing up, unaware that he would one day become the most famous drummer in the world.

Now that we had Ringo in the can, the next Beatle to be interviewed was Paul. We drove down to his studio in Sussex. In the corner of the room where we were going to do the interview was a double bass. While we were setting up, Paul saw me looking at it and explained that it had once belonged to Bill Black, the bass player in Elvis Presley's band. I had only ever seen the instrument in black-and-white footage but in real life it was gold in colour. Paul started playing the bass and told me to stand just in front of him. "If I am Bill Black, do you know who that makes you?"

I knew what Paul was saying. I was Elvis. I am sure that Paul does the same thing with everyone who turns up at his studio but I felt the hairs stand up on the back of my neck. I resisted the urge to burst into the first verse of *That's Alright Mama*. I didn't want to push my luck.

Paul was great and talked at length about growing up in Liverpool. We ended that first interview just as he was telling us about turning up at the Woolton Village Fete back in the summer of 1957, and meeting John Lennon for the first time. Sitting there and hearing Paul tell this story, it was hard to imagine what lay ahead and it started me thinking how different the world might have been if Paul had decided to stay at home that day.

The first time we interviewed George Harrison, he seemed the most reluctant of the three surviving Beatles in telling his side of the story.

I got the impression that he was the one who had the least fond memories of when he was 'fab', but what was obvious was that he wanted to set the record straight as to his role in the band and that during the making of the documentary he was not going to be 'the quiet Beatle'.

The one Beatle that we couldn't interview, of course, was John Lennon. Neil was, however, adamant that John would have an equal say in the documentary. I watched and listened to every interview that John had ever given, where he talked about his life before and during the Beatles years. We would then base our interviews with the other three around what we knew we had on archive from John.

Once we had done that first round of interviews, we decided the best way forward was to have each subsequent interview cover the period of each year that the band were together. We would tell them in advance that during the next interview we were going to be talking about 1962, for instance, and I would then provide a list of topics based on what happened that year.

Prior to interviewing Paul about 1965, he mentioned that he would like to be filmed on his boat. When I heard this, I wasn't going to argue. It would be nice to get out of the edit suite, and to hang out on a boat with 'Macca'. I was already checking to see if I had my Speedos with me and I had visions of sunbathing on the deck of a Sunseeker in San Tropez or somewhere just as exotic, when I was told that Paul's boat was in fact an old fishing vessel that he had moored down in Sussex. I put my disappointment to one side.

George suggested we film him in the garden of his home at Friar Park in Henley. He now seemed to be enjoying the interview situation and this was evident in the material that we were getting from him. But if we turned up to film and he wasn't feeling up for it, he would say so and we would pack away our equipment and rearrange for another day. The Beatles were paying the bills so that was their prerogative.

During February 1993, George decided that it would be a good idea to have a party to celebrate his 50th birthday, at Portmeirion Village in Wales (where, years earlier, the television series *The Prisoner* had been filmed). He suggested that while we were up there we could also do a couple of interviews. That sounded like a great idea.

The production team, together with Neil Aspinall and Derek Taylor (the former Beatles publicist and good friend of George), arrived at the Portmeirion Village Hotel. Later that same day, Jools arrived with various members of what would in years to come be the Jools Holland Big Band. We took over the whole of the village and the adjoining hotel.

On the Saturday night, Jools and his band set up in the ballroom and we had a party to celebrate George's birthday. It was a great night; probably not the best preparation for the interviews we were due to start filming the next day but it's not every day you get invited to a Beatle's birthday party.

The highlight of the evening was when George was invited on stage by Jools to play a couple of songs. One of the songs that George was going to perform was *Roll Over Beethoven*, a song that he had performed on record and on stage with the Beatles. George was happy to play guitar but didn't want to sing so he made a request that someone else do so. This was my chance to perform on stage with a Beatle. I was always willing to get up and sing and it wasn't like I didn't know the words to the song but I decided that I wouldn't do it as I was now working in television production. It remains one of the biggest regrets of my life.

"LET BOB DO IT"

On occasion, Jools Holland would not be available to conduct the interviews and it would not be possible to rearrange the dates to fit in with his schedule. Chips suggested I fill in, seeing as I had been setting the questions.

The first person I interviewed was Derek Taylor. Neil had decided Derek should be interviewed as he was one of the few people, aside from the Beatles themselves, who had been on the inside and witnessed first-hand the madness that went with being a Beatle. Also, like Neil, Derek was a loyal and trusted friend. I remember when I first met him; he could tell that I was a bit nervous about being in such exalted company and maybe feeling a bit unsure of my role in the proceedings. He took me to one side and told me, "It's really good to have some young people around the place." That helped calm my nerves and from that moment on, Derek and I got on really well.

Neil had also agreed to be interviewed, and rightly so. In my mind he was always the prime contender for the title of the 'fifth Beatle'; he had known the band when they were still schoolboys and had pretty much dedicated his life to them. There wasn't a day that went by when he wasn't 'working for the Beatles'. Neil could have sold his 'inside story' of the Beatles to the highest bidder a thousand times over, but that was not his style.

One day, I was chatting to Neil and he was telling me how he had learnt to copy the Beatles' autographs when they were touring and were too busy to sign after shows. These would then be handed out to fans. Neil said that many people who thought they had an original Beatle autograph had in fact an original 'Neil Aspinall Beatle autograph'. I handed Neil a piece of paper and said, "Go on then, show me." Neil took the pen, signed four autographs, and handed back the piece of paper. I couldn't believe it; they were the Beatles' autographs. I folded up the piece of paper and put it in my pocket. Neil said, "What do you think you are doing, Bob? Give me that back, that's worth a fortune." I gave him the piece of paper and he ripped it into a hundred pieces and dropped it in the bin. As always, protecting the legacy of the Beatles.

The first time I interviewed Neil, we had hired a house in Chiswick. When we turned up, the lady who owned it seemed a bit disappointed that it was not one of the Beatles that was going to be interviewed. Once we were set up to film, I pulled up a little stool to sit on. I was just about to ask my first question when the stool gave way and I was sitting on my arse on the floor. I heard Geoff say, "Let's cut there for a minute." The lady of the house came running into the room to see me sitting on the floor and the stool in pieces. She burst into tears and explained through her sobs that what I had sat on was not a stool but an 'occasional table'; a gift from her late husband.

I walked into the kitchen while Bryony Cranstoun, our production manager, comforted the distraught owner of the house. Neil followed me into the kitchen and I thought, 'That's it, I'm going to be fired.'

"Look, Neil, I am really sorry, I thought it was a stool," I said.

"I thought it was a stool too," he replied, "I very nearly sat on it five minutes before you did. Don't worry about it, where we come from we don't have 'occasional tables'."

That was typical of Neil; he knew how bad I felt and made light of it. I was given many a bollocking by him over the years when we would have a difference of opinion but he had a heart of gold and it was no wonder that the Beatles held him in such high esteem.

Everyone must have been happy with the job I had been doing so far and we got the message that Ringo wanted to be interviewed next in Los Angeles. Jools wasn't going to be able to make the trip so I was going over to do the interviews. The moment I stepped out of Los Angeles airport and into the sunshine, I fell in love with the place. California is the only place I have ever visited that was better in real life than it was in songs or in the movies.

On the morning that we were due to film our first interview with Ringo, we hired a Ford Mustang to drive down to the location in Malibu. When we got into the car and pulled away from the hotel, the radio was playing the Eagles doing their version of the Tom Waits song, *Ol' 55*. As we drove past the famous Beverley Hills hotel, I thought to myself, 'Here I am sitting in an open-top Mustang, driving down Sunset Boulevard, the sun's shining, the Eagles are playing on the radio, and I am going to interview Ringo Starr.' Ten years earlier I would have been sitting on the top deck of the number 35 bus, huddled into my greatcoat, heading to the shipyards in Wallsend, to spend my day welding in the double bottoms of a ship. I turned and looked at Geoff and it was as though he was reading my mind.

Ringo was in great spirits. He told us that he loved Los Angeles, and that when he first toured there with the Beatles he had fallen in love with the place and now spent a lot of his time there. During our interview I could see the Pacific Coast Highway winding behind him, and the Ocean rolling up onto the beach of Malibu.

On the morning of our second day, we filmed Ringo by the pool of the Sunset Tower Hotel then in the afternoon he said that he wanted to do some filming up in Griffith Park, a well-known tourist spot up in the Hollywood hills and the location of the famous knife fight in the movie *Rebel Without a Cause*.

Now, if you think the Beatles are famous in the UK, in America they are treated like gods. In fact, in LA they have radio stations that play nothing but Beatles records. With this in mind, I understood why Neil had decided it was a good idea that we have a security person with us, in the event that things got a bit out of hand.

Ringo and Neil were both wearing baseball caps and looked just like a couple of tourists wandering around the famous observatory. The fact that these two guys had a film crew following them wouldn't really attract much attention; this was Hollywood, after all, it was no big deal. We were eventually rumbled when someone noticed that there was a famous person being filmed; in fact, initially someone thought that it was the actor Harry Dean Stanton but one eagle-eyed guy pointed out that it was in fact Ringo Starr. Pretty soon, a small crowd had started following us so we decided we best get out of there. We jumped in the crew van and drove away. I was sat next to the security guy and asked him what he would have done if things had started getting out of hand. He pulled his shirt to one side to show me the gun that he had in a holster attached to his belt. "I would have used this." I was pleased we had got out of there when we did.

People have often asked me if I was ever nervous when interviewing the Beatles; it was not as though I had any sort of journalistic background or experience of anything similar, aside from a couple of times when I was presenting *The Colour Programme* many years earlier. This was very different. My interviewees were three of the most famous people on the planet but I approached it like I was having a conversation. My main concern was that I was getting the information we needed to make the documentary. It also helped that they were very down-to-earth and they wanted to talk.

What I found interesting was how they would often have conflicting answers to the same questions. We used this to our advantage during the editing process, in order to show how each of them would have different memories of specific events. This became a feature of what we were putting together and made for interesting viewing. Another thing I noticed was that once they started watching early cuts they began to see how we were using what they were saying, and they would tailor their replies accordingly. For instance, if we asked George a question and he was unsure of the answer he would say, "Ask Paul, he will know." We would use this in the edit, cutting from George saying this to Paul giving us the answer. They were steering the direction that the edit was taking. I doubt very much if this technique had ever been used before in a documentary.

Another thing I learned was that they would have quite clear memories of some of the smallest details but little or no recollection of some of the biggest events. One example was when I asked George about the time the Beatles played Shea Stadium during 1966, having been the first group ever to play the famous venue the previous year. I put the question to George of how it felt to be returning to play Shea for a second time. He replied, "What are you talking about? We didn't play Shea Stadium twice." Now, this wasn't some club gig in Hamburg; this was a world famous baseball stadium. I told George I'd seen the footage but he wasn't having it. He was in the band and I wasn't so who was I to tell him what gigs he did and didn't play? I asked Andy Mathews to play the archive of the 1966 concert. George watched, nodded his head, and said, "I am still convinced we didn't play there in '66."

On another occasion, Paul was telling us how nervous he was when he performed *Yesterday* solo on the Ed Sullivan show to a live audience of millions. During a break in filming I said to Neil Aspinall that Paul had performed *Yesterday* live in front of a studio audience but it was broadcast at a later date. I asked Neil what he thought I should do. Neil said, "If you want to tell Paul McCartney that he didn't perform his most famous song live to an audience of millions, then you can tell him." I decided not to contradict Paul. Sometimes it's best not to come across like too much of a smart-arse.

RUN FOR HOME

One of the perks of working in London was that every night was like a Friday night. After work, I would head up to Soho and have a drink in the Groucho Club; a private members club situated on Dean Street. On any given night you could be upstairs in the snooker room, playing doubles with the likes of Jarvis Cocker, Alex James from Blur, Stephen Fry, or Damien Hirst.

It would have been very easy to get sucked into that whole London scene but, as much as I enjoyed being there, it kept me sane knowing that come Friday I would be heading back to Newcastle. During those first couple of years while we were working on the *Anthology* there was not one weekend that I didn't head 'back home'.

One reason I couldn't wait to get back was that I had a new girlfriend called Karen Mays, who I had met in the Quay Club one night, prior to heading off to Riverside to see a Jools Holland gig. Karen was born and raised in Wallsend. She had a finely tuned bullshit detector and if she thought that I was getting above my station and was about to start talking about what I was up to in 'swingin' London' she would give me a look that said, 'Bob, you are sounding like a wanker.'

Karen never seemed to mind that, despite being away from home all week, come Friday night I would still want to hang out with my mates. Old habits die hard and Friday night was still 'lads' night out'. The lads were Nigel Steel, Tony 'Boot' Carnan, Gavin Kirkup, 'Big Al' Peacock and John 'the wild man of rock' Porteous. Every Friday night, we would gather at Gav's flat for a couple of liveners before hitting the bars and clubs on the Quayside. Never once did any of my mates ask me what I was up to in London. I am sure that if I started to talk about hanging out with members of Blur or Pulp they would either think that I was bullshitting or, even worse, getting big headed.

The fact that I was now earning decent money meant that at the age of thirty-five I was able to put a deposit down on my first house; a semi with a garden and a garage, on Brunton Park, a suburb in Gosforth. I loved that house. I wanted to put a plaque on the door that said 'Graceland' but Karen correctly pointed out that it would lower the tone of the area. I was also able to buy my first-ever electric guitar, twenty years after first gazing at them in magazines. I went for a Fender Telecaster, the same guitar that was played by one of my heroes, Joe Strummer from the Clash.

My upturn in fortunes was mirrored by that of my football team. Kevin Keegan had taken over as manager at Newcastle and had been instrumental in getting us promoted to the newly formed Premier League. Now that the club were back in the big time it was announced that part of the stadium would be given over to an exclusive 'platinum club'. I sent off my cheque for three thousand quid. For this I would be guaranteed a platinum club seat for ninety-nine years. I would also be given a special black-and-white blanket to keep my knees warm during those ten months of the year when it might get a bit nippy up there in the Toon.

I remembered turning up for the first game on the season, along with my mate Dave Armstrong, seeing my name on my padded seat and thinking to myself how I had come a long way since being sneaked through the turnstiles by my dad and freezing my arse off watching the game, sat on a stone barrier.

During the Toon's first attack I jumped up and felt a slap on the back of my head, I turned around to discover that sat directly behind me was Davey 'Animal' Hill. Animal weighed about sixteen stone, a giant of a man, and was going to be sat behind me for ninety-nine years; that was if I managed to even make it through the next ninety minutes. By the fourth game of the season we were on speaking terms. Davey had somehow got wind of the fact that I was working with Jools Holland on a Beatles documentary and he had a favour to ask. "Can you get me and wor lass into see Jools at the City Hall next Saturday?" I said I would see what I could do.

I asked Jools if he could sort it for me. "No problem," said Jools. "I will put him on the guest list." Now, as much as I had faith in Jools, he's a very busy man, and I dreaded the thought that it might slip his mind. The week following the gig I was back in my seat in the Platinum Club. At ten to three I looked up to see Animal coming up the stairs towards me. "Hey Bobby, come here." My heart was in my mouth. I had visions of him and his 'lass' turning up at the stage door and being told his name was not on the guest list. Not only would Animal's reputation be in tatters, pretty soon so would I. Animal grabbed me in a bear hug. "Thanks son, we got backstage and met Jools and the gig was great." Once I had freed myself from his grip he told me, "If you ever need a favour all you have got to do is ask." Thanks Jools, you saved my neck.

One weekend my sister Suzanne, who had recently got married and now had a daughter called Alba, rang me to say that my dad, who had remarried and was living in Scotland, was coming to visit her and had asked that I call around to see him. My first reaction was to say no but I thought this would be my chance to go around and show him that I had made something of myself.
When I arrived, he was there with a little boy who must have been around six years old. I presumed that this was his son. I asked the boy his name and he replied, "Bobby Smeaton." I couldn't fucking believe it; my dad had gone and called his son Bob. Seeing as he had been denying my existence to his new wife, why would he not? But I was furious. When he suggested we catch up for a drink later that night I did consider going along and taking 'Animal' Hill with me and cashing in his offer of 'a favour'. But in the end I decided not to. Our Tony accepted his offer and turned up at the pub with a load of his mates in case anything kicked off. I wasn't to know it but that day was the last time that I would see my dad.

THE SUMMER OF BRIT POP

The summer of 1994 was probably the greatest summer of my life. Tony Blair had just been elected as leader of the Labour Party, my football team were giving Manchester United a run for their money at the top of the Premier League, and Brit Pop was in full swing. I was also spending many a night at the Groucho Club, which it would appear was the centre of the Brit Pop universe. I would often find myself in conversation with various members of Blur and Oasis who, when I told them I was working with the Beatles, were never slow in acknowledging their love for the 'greatest Brit Pop band of all time'.

It wasn't just musicians who would fall under the spell of all things Beatle. One night I was sat talking to a girl who wasn't really paying that much attention to me. She kept looking over my shoulder, checking to see if anyone more interesting might be entering the club. Mid conversation, which was pretty much one-sided if the truth be told, I saw her eyes go wide and realised that she had spotted somebody famous heading our way. I turned around and looked over my shoulder to see Paul McCartney walking in. I was surprised to see Paul as this wasn't the sort of place he would normally hang out. As he passed, he spotted me and gave me a hug, and asked me how I was doing. Once Paul had gone on his way, suddenly me and my conversation became a lot more interesting. Thanks, Paul.

My mates from Newcastle would often come to visit me in London with the promise of a night at the Groucho and the prospect of meeting some 'famous people'. On one occasion, we were having a game of pool with Damien Hirst, who at the time was probably the most famous artist in the world and also a Beatles obsessive. I was deep in conversation with Damien and afterwards one of my mates, Gav, asked me who he was. I told him that he was a painter. Ten minutes later I overheard Gav ask Damien how much a painter in London would charge to decorate a living room.

One of the highlights of that summer was being introduced to Joe Strummer by the actor Keith Allen. For me, this was like meeting Elvis Presley. I was lost for words and just stuck out my hand and said, "Pleased to meet you, Joe." I was introduced to him a second time a month later by my friend Angela Taylor. She said she had never seen me so excited. What I noticed was that Joe's speaking voice sounded just like his singing voice and he spoke just like he sang, as if every word he said was important and delivered with the same passion that he put into performing on stage. When I told him I was working on the *Anthology* I was surprised when he said he was a massive Beatles fan and suggested that I tell Macca that he should get the Chemical Brothers to mix some of the Beatles tracks. He went as far as to write down his name and phone number on a piece of paper and told me to give him a call any time I wanted to talk about the Beatles. It remains one of my most treasured possessions.

By the autumn of that year we were over two years into the *Anthology* and had made rough cuts of all the programmes and sent these off to the Beatles to review. The first rough cut we sent began with a quote from Ringo: "My mother used to say that because I was born, the second world war started." We had, as planned, gone right back to the beginning and we were two hours into the story before they had even formed the band. In total, what we had assembled was running close to twenty hours. We knew that this story was never going to be told again, therefore we didn't want to leave out any detail. I asked Neil how long it might take for the Beatles to come back to us with all their comments. He said, "Don't hold your breath, but I wouldn't expect to hear anything before Christmas."

IN SUNSHINE OR IN SHADOW

Chips Chipperfield, the producer on the *Anthology*, had a friend called Julian Lloyd, who lived in Ireland and had an idea to make a film about the history of the song *Danny Boy*. Chips pitched the idea to ITV and they loved it. They wanted it to be broadcast in three months. The question was, could we squeeze it in during the time we were waiting to hear back from the Beatles? Geoff said he and Chips would produce it and I would be the director. It sounded great; it would be my first-ever credit as Director. I had the safety net of the same production team that were on the *Anthology*, including the cameraman Eugene O'Connor and the sound recordist Howie Nichol, who were both fantastic. I knew that they would have my back and do a great job for me.

We had no problem in getting contributors for the documentary. Politicians from both sides of the Irish political divide, as well as writers, sportsmen and musicians, were lined up to add their voices. Among these were: boxer Barry McGuigan, who would play the song at the end of his fights; the writer Brian Keenan who, when he was incarcerated for four years in Beirut, would sing the song to fellow prisoner, British journalist John McCarthy; and John Hume, the politician who was instrumental in trying to heal the rift between Catholics and Protestants, who was very vocal in the way that the song was able to bring people together, regardless of religious or political differences.

Having interviewed three Beatles, I felt pretty confident that I could now hold my own in any interview situation. The one interview that I was nervous about was Van Morrison. I had heard many stories about how much Van hated journalists, and how he was never happy being interviewed on camera. He was also renowned for giving one-word answers to questions, or not answering at all. Van had recently recorded *Danny Boy*, therefore I was sure that he would have something to say about the song and he had agreed to the interview, which in itself was a result.

When Van arrived to be filmed, I must admit I felt a bit scared; he didn't look very happy. The first question I asked was when had he first heard the song. He didn't even answer the question, he just shrugged his shoulders. I felt my stomach lurch. I then asked him what was his favourite version, to which he replied, "Too many to mention." This wasn't going very well. I had to play my ace. I told Van that my favourite version was by Ray Charles. I knew that Ray was Van's favourite singer. He started paying attention and for the first time made eye contact with me. Up to that point, he had been looking at a spot on the floor. He said, "Ray Charles? I have not heard Ray Charles' version, that is the version I would love to hear. If Ray Charles has recorded *Danny Boy* then that is my favourite version. Ray Charles could sing anything and I would love it. But the first time I heard it was by the McPeaks, when I was a young man growing up in Belfast."

Van was up and running and was great for the rest of the interview. I am sure that he would have left that day and gone out looking for Ray Charles' version of *Danny Boy*. I hope he found it. I had never heard Ray sing *Danny Boy* but, like most great singers, I am sure he did at some point!

The last filming day we had was with Eric Clapton. It had been some time since Eric had been interviewed on camera and it was also only a couple of years after his four-year-old son Conor had tragically died after falling through the open window of a high-rise apartment building in New York. When Eric arrived at Olympic Studios in Barnes, he seemed very subdued but told me that he loved the song and wanted to perform it as he felt it was the perfect song about loss and grief. Before we rolled the cameras, Eric said that he was going to play an instrumental version of *Danny Boy* as he thought he sounded like a club singer when he sang it. I was disappointed when he said this because even though he is a genius guitarist I also love his voice. Eric sat on a stool and played the song on his acoustic guitar. He only played it once and it was note-perfect. We held our breath as he played and when he finished there was total silence in the room. He didn't need the words to express what the song meant to him; the melody in itself was enough. We used Eric's performance to end the film.

Ten years after *Danny Boy* was broadcast on television I met the brilliant film director Jim Sheridan. Jim mentioned that he had seen the film when it was shown in Ireland and had sent a VHS tape of it to his friend, the actor Marlon Brando, as he knew that he too loved the song. He told me that having watched the film Brando called him to say that Clapton's version of the song had moved him to tears.

THE BEATLES ANTHOLOGY

By the time the Beatles had come back to us with all their comments, Neil had decided that the project was going to be called *The Beatles Anthology*.

Having watched the cut of the first programme, Paul's first comment was, "Can you take me out?" We couldn't believe it. This was a disaster. Without Paul there would be no documentary. He explained that he didn't like how he looked during his first interview set-up, and wanted to do a re-shoot. This was still a problem but not as bad as we had feared. We had a two-hour cut of that first programme and to unpick it and put it back together would take months. Paul said, "Don't worry, just tell me what I said and I will say the same thing again." And that was what we did. We gave Paul a script of all his comments, asked him the questions to elicit the answers, and Paul answered almost word-for-word. And he was right; he did look much better in the new set-up, in his black polo-neck sweater, rather than sat in an armchair in an open-neck shirt.

George also had a problem with parts of his first interview, which covered the early days. He felt he hadn't fully engaged in the project during the early stages and wanted to re-do some of the answers to a number of the questions. He told us the areas that he was uncomfortable with and we asked those questions again. What this demonstrated was that the guys in the band were now fully on board with what we were making and they too were grasping the enormity of the job at hand.

The comments regarding the content were few and far between and often came down to a difference of opinion, where we had included something we thought was important to the story but they didn't, or had missed something that they felt needed to be emphasised. They always had the final say but would still hear our argument if we felt strongly about something.

There was a bit of indecision about who had given the Beatles their name. Originally, we had a cut that gave credit for naming the band to John's friend and one-time Beatle bass guitarist, Stu Sutcliffe. In our first cut we suggested that Stu had possibly seen the film *The Wild One*, featuring Marlon Brando, whose character belonged to a gang called the Beetles, and suggested this name for the group. Yoko Ono insisted that it was John who had given the Beatles their name and that he had spoken about having a dream where he was visited by a man on a flaming pie and was told, "You are Beatles with an A." For a short while, the question of who named the group was split fifty-fifty between John Lennon and Stu Sutcliffe. In the final cut, John was credited with the naming of the band.

We also did a big section on Sgt Pepper. Each Beatle came back with the same comment: "Why have you made such a big thing about Pepper?" In their eyes it wasn't their greatest album. George, for instance, said that he much preferred *Rubber Soul* and *Revolver*.

To this day it is still assumed that we didn't use any voice-over on the *Beatles Anthology*, as Neil had insisted. But there was the odd occasion where we were lost for a bit of narrative to tell us where we were in the story or when we needed to turn a corner.

We had used a number of the audio recordings that the Beatles had made for *Saturday Club*; a radio programme hosted by Brian Matthews, broadcast on the BBC back in the 1960s. We got in touch with Brian and asked him if he would do voice-over for us as if he was on the radio talking about the Beatles back in the day. I wrote the script and we went along and met him. He sounded exactly the same as he had all those years ago. We built a set to look like a kid's bedroom, decorated with Beatles memorabilia, which would change with each passing year. We used the voice-over that Brian Matthews had done for us as if it was playing on the radio in the kid's bedroom. It worked perfectly.

We were aware that in the future, when people wanted to know the story of the Beatles it would be the *Anthology* that they would turn to. With this in mind, we made a decision early on that we didn't want to go overboard on any video effects as this would date the series. It would be like putting synthesisers on a music track; nothing dates as quickly as the latest sounds, and the same applied to visual FX. We did make a couple of concessions, one being to colourise some of the early black-and-white footage. At first we discussed colouring the earliest footage of the Beatles, when they played the Cavern Club. The problem with this clip was that there were no colour images that we could use for reference. We decided the best clip to colourise would be when they were filmed performing *All You Need is Love* in Abbey Road studios for the One World Television broadcast during 1967. We had access to photographs from the day so we were able to match the colours of the outfits that they were wearing. We sent the clip off and waited for its return. When it came back it looked fantastic. Even the most ardent Beatles fan, who thought they had seen everything, had never seen this performance in colour.

Aside from music that had already been recorded, there had been discussions about the Beatles recording some incidental music. Our expectations for this were totally surpassed when Neil and George turned up at the production office one day with a recording of a new song. Yoko had given the guys a rough demo of a song that John had written, called *Free as a Bird*. With Jeff Lyne producing, the other three Beatles had added an extra verse and their voices and instrumentation to John's demo. It had been over twenty-five years since there had been a new Beatles song and we were going to be given an exclusive playback of the finished track. It sounded fantastic.

Neil told us that we could not discuss the song with anyone. The seriousness of what Neil had said became evident later when I was leaving the edit suite for the day and he heard me singing the chorus and bollocked me. He told me to stop singing it in case someone might hear me and ask what I was singing.

THE WORLD IS WATCHING

In the fourth year working on the *Anthology*, it felt like we were hitting the home straight. Television broadcasters around the world had become aware of what we were making and were in discussions, with a view to broadcasting the *Anthology* as a television series. Neil told them they could have the series but were not allowed to change a single frame. Each broadcaster agreed that they would not have any editorial control; that would remain with the Beatles.

The pressure was really on during the next eight months. Not only did the Beatles have to have another round of viewings, we were also going to have to cut what was running at fourteen hours down to eight for the UK and six for America. Neil decided that the only way we were going to get it finished was if we were able to get the Beatles to come into the edit suite and watch each episode so we could address their comments while they were there with us.

One Friday afternoon, George arrived in his McLaren. As he was watching the cut he told us that, seeing the story laid out in front of him, he realised how much he had enjoyed those years when he was a Beatle, the laughs they had and how close they were, especially during the early years. He also commented that, unlike Bruce Springsteen and U2, and the current crop of big-name acts – although they were great and extremely successful – the Beatles were funny.

On this particular afternoon I was looking at my watch as I was booked on a flight back to Newcastle and due at Heathrow at 7.30. When George had finished watching the programme, I asked Chips if it was OK that I head off to catch the tube from Stamford Brook station up to Heathrow. Chips said, "Why don't you ask George to drop you off? He'll be driving that way on his journey back home to Henley." I told Chips that no way did I want to get in a car with George Harrison. Even though I had a feeling that George liked me and told me that I reminded him of his friend Michael Palin, which I guess I should have taken as a compliment, for some reason the thought of being in a car with a Beatle on my own made me nervous. Chips said, "OK then, get yourself away." I grabbed my bag and started jogging down to the tube. As I was about halfway there I heard the roar of a car engine behind me and turned around just as George in his McLaren pulled up at the kerb. It looked like I was going to get a lift after all. I jumped into the passenger seat then George looked at me and said, "Bob, there's something wrong with the car, it keeps cutting out."

I replied, "Can you not take it to Kwikfit?"

"What's Kwikfit?" I had never considered that George would never in his lifetime have reason to drive his car into Kwikfit.

"What do you want to do, George?"

He asked me to give him a push back to the production office. As I was pushing the car back, some local blokes were shouting and taking the piss out of me, suggesting that I should try putting petrol in next time. As I was struggling to push the car, they had no idea that the guy sat in the driver's seat was a Beatle. I walked into the office and Chips said, "What are you doing back?" I had a full sweat on, not only because I had just pushed a two-ton car containing a Beatle for about half a mile but also because it was looking like I might miss my plane. Chips very kindly booked me a cab to take me to Heathrow and I made the flight.

Having finally watched all the episodes, the Beatles decided there were still a couple of points that they would like to revisit. They felt they had not gone into enough detail on the recording of their songs and the role that record producer George Martin had played in their success. Rather than do another round of individual interviews, it was decided that they would be interviewed collectively. They had been filmed together at Friar Park the previous year and that had gone really well. When the guy from ABC television who had acquired the rights to screen the *Anthology* in America had seen this he had been ecstatic and commented that it would be fantastic if we could see more of that material. We would be killing two birds with one stone.

A date was set for the Beatles to get together at Abbey Road Studios. The plan was that we do a set-up of them together, with George Martin, listening to some of their multi-track recordings, and then for the three of them to be interviewed together. I had by this point interviewed each of them a number of times and felt pretty relaxed about it but to interview them collectively was a whole different ball game. Back in the day, they had been called the four-headed monster. Now I was going to be confronted by the three-headed monster. George knew that I had a job to do and kept steering the conversation back to my questions, while Ringo seemed to be leading the interview and Paul, strangely enough, seemed happy to take a back seat. I wasn't to know it at the time but 19th May 1995 was the last time the three of them would ever be interviewed together. Whatever else happens in my lifetime, no-one will ever be able to take away the fact that I was the last person ever to interview the three Beatles.

As we were nearing the end of the project, the question of how I was going to be credited reared its head. Geoff and Chips between them decided I should be credited as series director and writer. I had taken Geoff at his word about making the job whatever I wanted it to be, and also I had made *myself* look good in the process.

A couple of months before the series was due to be broadcast in America, it was announced to the world's press that the Beatles had recorded some new music which would be featured in a soon-to-be-released documentary series, *The Beatles Anthology*. From that moment on it was no longer a secret as to what had been going on in that white-washed building at the top of Wendell Road in Shepherd's Bush.

Chips asked if I fancied going to Los Angeles to do some press in the days leading up to the world premiere, and to watch the first couple of episodes being broadcast. I jumped at the chance. Why would I not want to go to LA and talk about the fruits of four years' labour? I mentioned to a couple of my mates in Newcastle that I was going to LA and asked if any of them fancied coming. Nigel Steel and Tony Boot said they were up for it.

The night before we flew out, we went to the Groucho for a few drinks. Not really the best preparation for a twelve-hour flight; we arrived at Heathrow the next morning a little worse for wear but still in high spirits.

By the time we got to the Mondrian Hotel in Los Angeles, we had hardly slept for forty-eight hours and we were feeling a little jaded. We didn't want to fall asleep and wake up in the middle of the night so decided that the best thing to do was to try and stay awake until what would be bedtime in California. Up the road from our hotel on Sunset Boulevard was the world-famous strip club, The Body Shop. This was a frequent hang-out of the likes of Motley Crew and Guns N' Roses, and we used that as our excuse to go and check it out. When we turned up and the guy on the door heard our English accents, he must have seen dollar signs; he welcomed us into the club and gave us a seat in prime position, right near the front of the stage. We ordered a round of drinks and waited for the show to begin. Within half an hour, we were being escorted out of the club. We had all fallen asleep in our beers. You can take the boys out of Newcastle but even the sight of a bunch of scantily-clad California Girls was not going to keep them awake.

On the evening of Sunday 19th November 1995, we gathered around the television in the bar of the hotel to watch the world premiere of the first episode of *The Beatles Anthology*. At the end, as the credits rolled and my name appeared, Tony Boot turned to me and said, "So that's what you've been doing for the past four years."

When I returned to the UK, Neil told me that Bob Dylan had been in touch to say that he had watched the *Anthology* and that there might be a chance that we could do his story next. George Harrison also mentioned that maybe the time was right to do his post-Beatles story.

Both of these prospects were exciting but as it turned out Martin Scorsese ended up doing documentaries on both Dylan and George.

Once the series had been broadcast we spent close to a year assembling the long-form video versions. When they were finished, George came into the production office for one final viewing. As he was leaving, I followed him onto the street. I told him it had been a privilege working on the series and as I would probably never see him again, I wanted to say thank you. George replied that we might not meet again in this life but maybe we would in the next.

That Christmas, I received a handwritten card from Paul that said 'thanks for all that hard graft, it was a long and winding but worth it in the end road', alongside a beautiful Silver Cross fountain pen that was inscribed 'The Beatles Anthology lots of love from Paul and Linda'.

Ringo sent a fax to the office saying how he would like to thank *everyone* for all their hard work. George also sent a thank you note, together with a bottle of vintage Dom Perignon. When I took the bottle home to Newcastle I told Karen that I would open it when Newcastle United won a major trophy or when we had our first child, whichever came first.

BACK ON THE QUAYSIDE

The Beatles Anthology was over. It had been one hell of an adventure, and probably the greatest experience of my life. It felt strange to wake up on a Monday morning and not be packing my bag in preparation for the trip to London. Chips and I still spoke on the phone every day and he was convinced that because the *Anthology* had received great reviews we would be able to capitalise on its success and before long be offered more work off the back of it.

At first I enjoyed having the time off but within a couple of months I found myself for the first time in almost five years with nothing to do.

Dave Holly, my old theatrical agent, rang and asked if I was up for doing some acting work, as Tyne Tees had been in touch to check if I was available to audition for a soap opera called *Quayside*. I went along and met the director, Matthew Robinson, and read for the part of a journalist called Dan Caffrey. I must have done OK as I was offered the role and told that filming the first of eight episodes would begin in two weeks.

I wasn't really sure if I wanted to go back to acting as I thought I might find a niche for myself making music documentaries but the offers of more documentary work hadn't materialised so I accepted the *Quayside* job. I loved every minute of it. Each morning, I would jump into my car and drive down to the film set on Team Valley trading estate and then drive back home in the evening. The cast and crew were great; all I had to do was turn up and say my lines. There was none of the pressure that I had been under for the past five years and I loved being back at home full-time.

As much as I had loved working on *Quayside* and thought it wasn't a bad first series, my opinion wasn't shared by the viewing public. They hated it. It was absolutely slated and after the first couple of episodes no-one was watching it. Tyne Tees had decided to broadcast it at the same time as the BBC's *EastEnders*, the biggest show on television. We didn't stand a chance.

Halfway through the screening of the first series, we were told by the producers that Tyne Tees had decided not to commission a second series. That was pretty much the end of my acting career.

AND THE WINNERS ARE

One bright spot on the horizon was that awards season was coming up, in the UK and in America. *The Beatles Anthology* had been nominated for a BAFTA for best documentary series and for best sound and editing. In America it was nominated for an Emmy for outstanding information series, and in the Grammys for best long-form music video. The first award ceremony was the BAFTAs, which were held at the Hilton Hotel on Park Lane in London. We didn't win best documentary series but Andy Mathews and Howie Nichol picked up the BAFTA for best sound. We were hoping to go one better when, during September of that same year, Geoff, Andy and I headed out to California for the Emmy awards.

On the evening before the awards we were sat in the bar of the Sunset Marquis hotel when in walked my friend from Newcastle, John 'the wild man of rock' Porteous. John announced that he had just been on a twenty-two-hour flight that eventually deposited him in Los Angeles. He told me that he didn't want to miss my big night at the Emmys.

The Emmys are the television equivalent of the Oscars and to be nominated was a big deal. We all piled into a stretch limo, in our dinner jackets and black ties, and headed over to the Civic Auditorium in Pasadena. We were up against a series about lost civilisations and one about the secret life of plants. In the end we were beaten by the lost civilisations. We were all a bit disappointed that we hadn't won and Geoff was really pissed off and correct in his observation that we had been placed in the wrong category. How many hit records had the lost civilisations had? Not as many as the Beatles, that was for sure. Even so, just to have been nominated was a cause for celebration. John Porteous and I didn't go to bed that night and hoped that we would have better luck next time, at the Grammys.

Neil, Chips, Geoff and I had been nominated for a Grammy and Chips asked who was up for going to the award ceremony in New York. Chips didn't like awards dos and had already decided he didn't want to go; Geoff didn't want to because of the disappointment of not winning an Emmy; Neil was too busy dealing with Beatles business to make the journey. When I found out that the awards were being held at Madison Square Garden, for me that was reason to go in itself. I had never been there and the chance to go and possibly pick up a Grammy was too good to pass by. John Porteous was also up for the trip.

John and I checked into the Paramount Hotel, just off Times Square, and booked a stretch limo to take us to the venue. 'The Garden' was less than a mile away and we had to be there for five o'clock so we booked our ride for four-thirty. At four-fifty we had travelled three blocks; the traffic was bumper-to-bumper rush hour in central Manhattan. With ten blocks still to go, we jumped out of the limo and made a run for the venue. We got into our seats just as they were announcing the winner for the best spoken word album; this was Hillary Clinton, whose husband Bill was the US president at the time. She made a short speech and left the stage.

Next up was the award that we were up for, best long-form music video. The award was going to be presented by Bill Ward, the drummer from Black Sabbath. I took that as a good sign as Bill was a Brit and Sabbath had been one of my favourite bands when I was a kid. What wasn't in our favour was that two of the other nominees were Bruce Springsteen and Bon Jovi, who hailed from just down the road, in New Jersey. My heart was exploding in my chest as Bill opened the envelope and announced, "The winners are Neil Aspinall, Geoff Wonfor, Chips Chipperfield and Bob Smeaton for *The Beatles Anthology*." Never mind trying to be cool, I was jumping up and down as I ran down the aisle and onto the stage. I couldn't believe it. Bob Smeaton, a former welder from Benwell, was on stage at Madison Square Garden. I might not have made it as a rock star but at that moment in time winning a Grammy felt like the next best thing to having a number one record.

I hadn't prepared a speech. I just said the first thing that came into my head; I mentioned the journey from Newcastle to New York and thanked the Beatles and the rest of the people who had worked on the *Anthology*. I would have stayed up there all night, given the chance. If they had asked me to do a song, I would have sung one. The next thing I knew, I was being escorted off the stage.

When I got backstage, I bumped into Hillary Clinton and shook her hand, and told her how much I liked her speech and that I was going to buy her album when I got back to the UK. I was then ushered into a room where a photograph was taken of me proudly holding my award, then someone came along and took the award from me and gave me a piece of card that said 'Winner Long Form Video'.

I was then taken to meet the world's press. Having just been presented with Hillary Clinton, they were probably hoping the next person to stand in front of them would be Bruce Springsteen or Eric Clapton; they looked a bit disappointed when it was me.

After the briefest of interviews, I rolled up my piece of card, stuffed it into the jacket of my tuxedo, and headed back to my seat to watch the rest of the ceremony, which was beamed to a television audience of twenty million.

When the show was over I went off to look for a pay phone to call my mam back home in Newcastle.

I eventually found a phone, deep in the bowels of Madison Square Garden. I didn't have any quarters so I dialled the operator and asked her if she could place a call to my mam and ask if she could take a reverse-charge call. I heard my mam answer the phone and the operator saying, "Hello, will you take a collect call from New York?"

"I don't know anyone in New York," replied my mam.

I shouted down the phone, "It's me, Ma, Bobby," even though she couldn't hear me. Eventually, the operator was able to persuade her to take the call.

"It's me, Mam, we won a Grammy."

To which she replied, "What time is it there, son?"

"Eleven o'clock at night, Mam."

"Eleven o'clock at night, eeh that's fantastic, it's four o'clock in the morning here." My mam was more impressed by the time difference than any award that her son had won.

John and I headed to the after-show party, in some big flash hotel just off Madison Avenue. John took great delight in telling anyone that would listen that his mate Bob had 'won a Grammy'. This was only in the event that they had not noticed the card that read 'Winner Long Form Video' that was now pinned to the lapel of my tux. I spent a great deal of time at the party looking for Bruce Springsteen, to offer my commiserations for not having won in our category, and my congratulations for having won with his *Ghost of Tom Joad* album. I was also hoping that he might remember me from the impromptu duet we had performed back in 1981. I never did find Bruce.

Having just about cleared the bar, John and I were starting to flag. He suggested a place in Greenwich village where he reckoned we could get some sustenance that would allow us to continue our evening. We jumped into a yellow cab and headed down to the Burrito Bar, where sure enough we were able to secure the necessary refreshments that allowed us to continue our celebrations back at our hotel into the wee small hours of the morning. We didn't bother going to bed as we knew sleep would be out of the question, due to a mixture of excitement, jet lag and the after-effects of our visit to the Burrito Bar. Also, we had an early flight to catch in the morning.

As we were packing our bags, I mentioned to John that we had better dispose of what remained of our 'take-away' as we didn't want to be carrying that on the plane with us. John agreed and disappeared into the hotel bathroom to get rid of it. During the cab ride from Manhattan out to the airport, John got into an animated conversation with our Indian cab driver who, upon realising that we were English, had asked if we liked cricket. I was not a fan of cricket so for close to two hours I listened to what was pretty much a one-sided conversation about the beauty of the game, John very much leading the charge.

When we arrived at JFK, as we got our bags out of the back of the cab, John said a lengthy goodbye to his new friend and told him that if he ever visited Newcastle to be sure to get in touch.

"Bloody hell, John, I never realised you were such a big fan of cricket," I said.

"I'm not," said John. "Actually, Bob, I've got a confession to make. You know that stuff I was meant to flush down the toilet? I didn't want to waste it so I did it all in before we left the hotel."

"Really, John?" I replied. "I would never have guessed."

It was going to be a long journey home.

When we checked in for our flight, thanks to the kindness of the good people at Apple, I was flying back business class, which meant I would not be sitting next to John. I felt sorry for the unfortunate passenger who had drawn that short straw. One thing was certain: with John sat next to them they wouldn't be getting much sleep during the next seven hours.

I would like to say that I arrived back in Newcastle proudly clutching my Grammy but, in fact, when my flight touched down the award was still back in New York, waiting to be inscribed. It would be a number of weeks before it turned up and found pride of place on my mantelpiece. But I did return to discover that I had made page two of the *Evening Chronicle*. There I was, standing in my tuxedo, proudly clutching my Grammy. The headline read something along the lines of 'Geordie actor from flop soap opera makes it big in America'. The piece went on to say how I had been given the award for my work on *The Beatles Anthology* and how this would no doubt go some way to compensate for the fact that *Quayside* had not been commissioned for a second series because no one had watched it. Still, it made my mam really happy to see her son in the newspaper; so much so that she tore out the article and taped it to her wall. Three months later, it was still there!

The day after my triumphant return home, my sister Suzanne presented me with a poem that she had written and I must admit that when I read it, it brought a tear to my eye.

My Brother. My Hero

I bet your palms were hot and clammy
the evening that you won your Grammy.
Up on stage so glad and proud
listening to them all clap loud

In the newspaper, page two
I saw the photograph of you,
could not be taken for another,
It's really him it's my big brother

Saw the message in your eye
Its meaning made me want to cry,
and so I did great pride inside
I looked at you and cried, and cried

I recalled all the things you've done,
the obstacles you've overcome.
The times when all your luck was gone,
stuck to your guns, and just forged on.

Those early mornings in the rain,
just wishing you could start again.
Waiting for the 38
to take you to the shipyard gate
(*Which inevitably was always late*)

Home again you would not dare
to speak because the old man's there
not a single word was said

for fear he'd rise and punch your head.

You won't get anywhere he said
(*at times we all wished he was dead*)
from every wall his voice would boom
you'd go upstairs stay in your room.

I was quite young and could not see
all of the pain and misery
he'd made you feel along the way
it's no surprise you couldn't stay.

You moved out, I do recall
removed your posters from your wall
and even though despite your rage
you kindly left me Jimmy Page.

I must have been about eleven
when you introduced me to 'Stairway to Heaven'
Perhaps the words moved you along....
And made you realise you could change the road that you were
travelling on

And change you did you just got going,
creative juices started flowing
up on stage, long hair a-flying,
teenage girls, worked up and crying.

The Hooray boys and girls would come,
get drunk and dance, enjoy the fun.
It really was the saddest day
when you put your mike away.

You worked hard when things got tough,
just bit your lip, did not give up.

Most folk wished they had what you had,
one step back but three steps forward

Time moves on, what can I say?
Here I am standing today,
filled with pride and admiration,
raise my cup in celebration.

No-one deserves this honour more,
you've worked hard to open every door.
My guiding light, a shining star,
My Brother, My Hero, that's who you are.

Sue. 28.2.97

Me and our Sue hadn't really seen a lot of each other over the past few years; she now had another daughter, Esme, and we had drifted apart. On the occasions that we did see each other we had never really discussed what I was up to. And we never talked about what it was like for us when we were growing up, or that she was even aware of what I had been through, but in the poem that she wrote she had pretty much summed up my life to that point.

Looking mean and moody in an advert for *Famous for 15 Minutes*.

Andy Matthews, me and Geoff Wonfor in the edit suite in
Shepherd's Bush.

Me and Paul.

With George outside the edit suite.

With Ringo in Malibu along with the red Mustang we hired.

With the King on the boardwalk in Santa Monica.

With Neil Aspinall and Chips Chipperfield in Portmeirion for George's 50th Birthday Party.

Backstage at Madison Square Garden.

With John Porteous at the Grammys.

LIFE AFTER BEATLES

WHO'S NEXT?

I hadn't seen or heard from Geoff since returning from the Grammys ceremony. I knew that he was working with Andy Mathews, on the first project that he had not got me on board in around ten years. Maybe he thought I was ready to start doing stuff on my own. During the twenty years since we had met we'd had our rows and our ups and downs but I owed so much to him and, more than anything else, he was one of my best mates and I loved him. As I would often tell anyone who would listen, I would have never been anywhere near the *Anthology* had it not been for him.

How do you follow working with the 'greatest group of all time'? I didn't know how to answer this question. I had hoped that being credited as series director and writer on the *Anthology*, and having won a Grammy, might have signalled the start of a career making music documentaries but a year after finishing, the deluge of offers that I was hoping for hadn't come my way.

It was a bloke called John McDermott who eventually provided the answer as to what would be next, and how to follow the 'most famous group of all time'. In spring 1998, Chips got in touch to tell me that John had called to ask if we would be interested in making a documentary that he was going to executive-produce. John wanted to bring me on board as director, and Chips and Neil Aspinall as producers. We were going to make a documentary about the 'greatest guitarist of all time', Jimi Hendrix.

John was working for Experience Hendrix – the company which was run by Jimi's sister, Janie. He explained that they wanted to make a film based around Jimi's short-lived Band of Gypsys. The group had performed fewer than a handful of gigs, the most famous being at the Fillmore East in New York. According to John, both the band and the gigs were legendary. He had just gained access to footage that was shot at the shows and he thought this material could form the basis of the documentary.

John showed the footage to me, Chips and Neil. My heart sank. It was really grainy black-and-white early video footage. If that was all we had to work with, it would be a struggle. Neil felt the same way and voiced this opinion to John, pointing out that not only did we not have great archive footage, we didn't have the equivalent of John, Paul, George and Ringo to provide the narrative for the story. Hendrix had died back in 1970, less than a year after the concert was filmed, and had never really spoken on film or tape about the Band of Gypsys. It was going to be a big ask.

John McDermott was convinced that, even without being able to interview the 'main man', and with the questionable quality of the footage we had to work with, the story was worth telling. Also, he was prepared to put his money where his mouth was and finance the film. Neil and Chips asked me what I thought and I said, "I think John is right, we have the potential here to make a really great film." It was a total bluff on my behalf; my guts were already churning, but I was desperate to be working again.

We might not have been able to interview Hendrix but the other two guys who were in the band with him - bassist Billy Cox and drummer Buddy Miles - were still alive and up for up being interviewed, as were Jimi's former band members from the Experience; Noel Redding and Mitch Mitchell. John said that we would also be able to film other musicians and friends of Jimi's to shed light on why the Band of Gypsys were such an important band.

As I discovered during my initial research before we began filming, prior to forming this band, Hendrix had been under pressure from the Black Panthers to become more of a voice for black people in America.

As it transpired, both his new band mates, Billy Cox and Buddy Miles, were black musicians and Jimi's desire to work with this new line-up was also partly to do with wanting to take his music in a different direction to what he had done with the Experience, and to reach a black audience. I was beginning to see why John McDermott wanted this story be told.

Having filmed with Billy Cox and Buddy Miles in uptown New York, we travelled down to the East Village to film at Electric Lady Studios. Here we were going to be shooting some additional material with Billy, along with Eddie Kramer, who had been the recording engineer on all of Hendrix's albums. When I was in the studio with Billy, I kept talking to Eddie via the talkback while has was in the control room but he wouldn't answer me. I started to get the impression that he didn't like me. I eventually walked into the control room and asked him if he had a problem. Eddie nearly jumped out of his skin. What had happened was he thought that the voice that was asking him if he was 'ready to roll' was Chas Chandler, Jimi's former record producer and manager, who was on the multi-track tapes that he was listening to. Chas, like me, spoke with a Geordie accent and when Eddie played me the tape of Chas talking, we did sound very similar. To this day, Eddie says it still freaks him out when I ask him to 'roll the tapes'.

The last leg of filming was going to be in Los Angeles. I was always excited about the prospect of going to LA.

One of the interviews that we had set up was with Slash, the guitarist from Guns N' Roses. I wanted to find out what it was about Hendrix that so appealed to Slash when he was a young kid growing up in Stoke-on-Trent back in the UK. My first question was, "Tell me, Slash, what was it about Hendrix that appealed to a young white kid growing up in Stoke-on-Trent?" To which he replied, "Well, first, can I say that I wasn't a young 'white kid' growing up in Stoke-on-Trent. I am not white." I nearly fell through the floor. I had not realised that Slash was mixed race. I thought I had blown it but Slash was really cool and laughed it off, and in fact invited me along to a Paul Rodgers gig that night at the House of Blues on the Sunset Strip, where he was going to get up and play a few songs with the former Free front man. There were no hard feelings, and I was going to get to watch one of my former heroes, Paul Rodgers, doing a show in LA. It didn't get any better than this.

That night after the gig, I was back at Le Parc Hotel and awoke in the middle of the night. I looked at the digital clock by the side of my bed, it was 3.30 a.m. and for the first time ever I got 'the fear'. I started thinking that I was not getting the material that I needed to make the film and that Experience Hendrix had put up all of this money to pay for something that I was not going to be able to deliver. I was petrified. I realised that I no longer had Geoff Wonfor to cover my back and the buck stopped with me. I had visions of being sent to prison, having signed a contract that meant I had to deliver a film, and I had already spent half of the budget. I decided that first thing the next morning I was going to call Chips back in London and tell him I could not deliver what he had asked and ask him to apologise to John McDermott on my behalf. I would give him back the money that I had been paid to date.

I started having visions of having to return to the shipyards and explain to my workmates that I was only back on a temporary basis. I lay on my bed, staring at the ceiling, and tried my best to slow down my heart, which was beating so fast I thought I was going to have a heart attack. Eventually, the sun came up, my heart rate slowed, and I decided against calling Chips. The edit was due to start in a week and I would be working with a new editor called Julian Caidan. He and I would try our best to make something with the material that we had filmed. I was scared.

Around four weeks into the edit, however, I started to feel that it was coming together. I sent John a cut of around 45 minutes of what we had assembled so far. John called me as soon as he got the tape and told me, "It's brilliant, it's much better than I could ever have imagined." After that phone call from John, for the first time in around six weeks I got a decent night's sleep and no longer woke myself up just as I was scrambling under the gates at Swan Hunter's Shipyards.

THE BAND

I was just about finishing the edit on the Hendrix documentary when I got a call from Caroline Thomas, a television producer who wanted me to meet her boss, to discuss a potential project. Nick de Grunwald was a really smart guy; his production company was called Isis, which at the time was not a name that was associated with a terrorist organisation but another name given to the river Thames at the point where it flows through the city of Oxford. It was also the name of the student magazine at Oxford University. *Isis* also happened to be the name of a Bob Dylan song, which seemed fitting as Nick wanted to speak to me about possibly directing a documentary that would feature Bob's former backing group, the Band. Nick explained that he was making a series called *Classic Albums*, which looked in detail – as the title would suggest – at the making of classic albums, and was in the process of commencing production on a film about the Band's second album. This album, as I would later discover, would commonly be referred to as their 'Brown Album'. Nick asked if I thought it might be something I would like to direct, and if I would be up for writing a treatment to outline how I would make the film.

I told Nick that I was not really aware of the Band, or their second album; in fact, at the time I wasn't really a massive Dylan fan, but that I would go away and read up on them, listen to the album, and then write a treatment. This meant that I would be outlining my 'vision' for the film. I set about doing my research.

Over the next two weeks, I read a couple of books that had been written about the Band; one by Barney Hoskyns called *Across the Great Divide* and another by Levon Helm, who was the drummer in the Band. Barney's book was fantastic and Levon's was also a good source of information. But the real revelation was the music. How had I gone all these years and not heard this album? I was aware of a couple of songs, *The Night They Drove Old Dixie Down* and *Rag Mama Rag*, but the album as a whole was the best thing I had heard in ages. The songs were great and the singing was fantastic; they had three great vocalists and the music was like nothing I had heard before. For a week, I was listening to that album continuously. I couldn't believe how great it was. I began to understand why many musicians credited them as the greatest band of all time. I then went out and bought all their other albums and played them to death; they were even responsible for making me go out and buy a bunch of Dylan albums, and so began my love affair with all things Bob. I was so excited, I had to make this documentary. I wrote a two-page treatment and took it with me to have another meeting with Nick.

Nick read my treatment and seemed disappointed that I had only written two pages. "Is this all I get from the guy who was the writer on the *Beatles Anthology?*"

I told him in no uncertain terms that I had spent time in recording studios; I had made records myself; I knew what a mixing desk did; I was aware of how many microphones to place on a drum kit to get the best sound; I knew what a middle eight was, and the difference between the sound of a Fender Strat and a Gibson Les Paul. The reason I knew all this was because I had been in a band for fifteen years and on top of that I had just won a Grammy for *The Beatles Anthology*. If he wanted a thesis on the Band then he could get someone else to write it but if he wanted a great documentary then I was the man for the job. I'm sure Nick didn't mean to offend, but I was offended. I got up and started walking out of his office. Nick called me back and offered me the job.

I had convinced Nick that I was the right man but I was really scared. This would be the first time that I would be working with people I didn't know. On the Beatles and Hendrix jobs, Neil and Chips had my back, as did the cameraman, Eugene. On this occasion I didn't know any of the production team and I would have to bring on board a camera and sound crew that I had never worked with before so there would be no familiar faces. I got in touch with my old pal Geoff Wonfor and asked for his advice. I think he was quite pleased that I had reached out to him. He told me that there were hundreds of cameramen and soundmen who would do a good job for me, but that I should choose people who I felt I would be able to get along with and who would be there for me if things ever got a bit tricky. I ended up bringing on board Steve Tickner and Tim Fraser, who seemed like decent blokes and liked a laugh.

Once I had assembled my crew, I got in touch with George Harrison. I remembered him mentioning the Band when we were making the *Anthology*, and how he had hung out with them in Woodstock prior to making the Beatles' *Let It Be* album. I asked him if he would be up for doing an interview. He said he had only just recently done an interview about the Band for another documentary series but I was welcome to use that. He went on to say, "You should speak to Eric as he is also a massive fan." I gathered that George meant Eric Clapton. I got in touch with Eric and I mentioned that we had met when we had made the *Danny Boy* film. He told me that he also had just done an interview about the Band but I was welcome to use that. I hadn't even started filming yet and we already had George Harrison and Eric Clapton in the can. Things were looking good.

I called Levon Helm and discussed how best we would approach the filming with him. Levon told me that we could film with him at his barn out in Woodstock. He explained this was where he lived and it also housed all of his equipment. He also had a recording studio there so we could go through the multi-track tapes of the album. He offered to speak to his bandmates, Rick Danko and Garth Hudson, and persuade them to come along to be filmed at this location. Nothing seemed to be too much of a problem. He signed off by telling me how much he was looking forward to meeting me and my film crew and that he would have a drink waiting for us.

We got to Woodstock the night before we were due to film up at Levon's barn. I called Garth Hudson and asked him if he would be available to turn up at Levon's place around twelve the following day. I then put a call in to Rick Danko and asked if he could be there at around three. Both of them agreed and Rick said how much he was looking forward to it.

The next day, we arrived at Levon's barn. He came out in his dressing gown to meet us and asked if we would like a drink; he was true to his word. We got set up and started listening to the multi-track tapes of the album, alongside the record's producer, John Simon. Levon was in great spirits but as we were highlighting the contribution made by each member of the band, he never once pushed up the fader that featured Robbie Robertson's guitars, nor did he at any time mention Robbie's name. It was as if Robbie didn't exist. There was bad blood there because Robbie had written most of the Band's biggest songs and had never shared the songwriting royalties with the other guys. Hearing those tapes of the album, it was obvious you could not have made that record with any other musicians, they were *The Band*. But it appeared that now they were the Band only in name and as far as Levon was concerned they certainly were no longer a 'band of brothers'.

Rick Danko arrived later that day, as arranged. He looked nothing like the handsome young guy that I had seen in pictures and on film; he had almost doubled in size and had a bad case of the shakes. Rick had a reputation for being a guy who liked a good time, and the good times had taken their toll on him. But he was really friendly and still had a twinkle in his eye. Even though he looked very different from the guy who had contributed so much to the sound of the band, when he started to sing it choked me up. If I closed my eyes, he sounded just like he did on the multi-track tapes that we had just been listening to, which were recorded thirty years earlier, back in 1969.

It had been a great day. My only disappointment was that Garth Hudson had not turned up. I had heard that he was a very private man and he had mentioned when I had spoken to him that he didn't relish the idea of being filmed, so there was always the chance he wouldn't show.

Around ten p.m., we started packing our filming gear. We had packed away most of our equipment when the door to the barn swung open and in walked Garth. Under one arm he was carrying a saxophone and under the other a keyboard. The first thing Garth said was, "Sorry, I'm early." It transpired that in Garth's world, twelve could only mean midnight, never midday.

Garth set up his keyboards and started to play. I was mesmerised. I had never seen or heard anything like this in all my life. John Simon was standing next to me and said, "You should be filming this." I quickly told Steve the cameramen to turn over and we filmed Garth for around fifteen minutes while he played this crazy keyboard piece. When he stopped he said, "Well, I guess that's it, then." He never spoke another word, just packed up his instruments and walked out of the door. That was Garth Hudson, genius.

Having filmed with Levon, Rick and Garth, we flew down to Los Angeles to film with Robbie Robertson. We were going to be filming him in a recording studio that he had requested and upon arrival it was obvious from the moment we turned up that this was not the informal set-up we had experienced at Levon's barn out in Woodstock. We loaded in our equipment and sat in reception, waiting for Robbie Robertson to arrive.

We had been waiting for around ten minutes when a policeman walked in and asked who was the owner of the vehicle that was parked outside. Caroline Thomas, the producer of the documentary, stepped forward. The policeman pulled out his handcuffs and told her she was under arrest for parking illegally. She went white. He then put the handcuffs on her, made her sit in a chair, and started doing a strip down to his underwear. As it turned out, it was her birthday. One of the girls on the crew thought it would be a laugh to have a strip-a-gram show up at the studio and surprise her.

Just after the cop had finished his act and put his uniform back on, Robbie Robertson walked in the door. Had he arrived five minutes earlier, he would have been confronted by an almost naked man straddling the producer of the documentary. I made a mental note to have a word with the person responsible for the birthday surprise once we had finished filming.

Robbie was totally different to the band members we had left behind in Woodstock. I would never have imagined that this guy would have been in a band with those other three. Robbie was dressed in a two-piece suit and open-neck shirt. He looked like a Hollywood movie star and with him it was all business. He asked if he could have a word with me before we started filming and went on to explain that he wasn't feeling too great; he felt like he was going to be sick and was having dizzy spells, and we might have to stop the filming if he didn't improve. There wasn't much I could say to this aside from, "Let's give it a go and get what we can."

We started with the sit-down interview. Robbie was a great raconteur and his recall of the early days of the group, and the time they had spent backing Bob Dylan when he went electric, was encyclopaedic. He then sat at the piano and talked us through the writing of a number of his classic songs, including *The Night They Drove Old Dixie Down*. When Robbie played the introduction to this song then started to sing it, I held my breath. I had heard the song sung by Levon Helm hundreds of times but I had never heard it sung by the guy who wrote it. And when we were going through the multi-track tapes, he knew where every note was played on each of the songs. When he highlighted the vocals of Richard Manuel, the one member of the Band who was no longer alive, I am sure he wiped a tear from his eye. Robbie want to great lengths to emphasise the contribution the other four guys had played in making it a Classic Album.

As we were packing up to leave, I realised that there had been no sign of the sickness that Robbie had mentioned when he first arrived. This was the guy who had written a song called *Stage Fright*, having famously suffered from this prior to the Band giving their first live performance in support of their second album; something that I would later reference in the documentary. I am no psychologist, and have no idea of what goes on in the head of Robbie Robertson, but my bet was that he had rehearsed and prepared for the day's filming with us in the same way that he would have done for a gig, and just like had happened thirty years earlier, was suffering from a bit of stage fright.

At the end of that day's filming, I was certain that we had the makings of a great documentary. In fact, I was so pleased with what we had got from Robbie that I went easy on the production person who thought it was a good idea to book the strip-a-gram.

We finished the documentary and it had turned out as well as I had hoped. The section where Garth turned up and played his keyboards brought a broad smile to the face of everyone that watched it. My only disappointment was that when we showed it to Levon he came back with a comment saying that he thought that I had "laid a funeral wreath on the Band's career". He suggested that Robbie Robertson had more of an input into how the documentary turned out than any of the other members, but that wasn't the case. Robbie had been sent a cut of the finished film, just like the other guys, and he thought it was great. I guess anything we showed Levon that featured Robbie Robertson wouldn't have gone down well.

Many years later, during April 2012, I was filming a performance by English new wave band Squeeze at the Fillmore West in San Francisco. The Fillmore is just down the road from the Winterland Ballrooom, the venue where the Band had played their last-ever performance, which was turned into the legendary Martin Scorsese film *The Last Waltz*. Halfway through the day, I got a message on my mobile phone saying that Levon Helm had died.

The documentary I made on the Band remains one of my favourites and, aside from *The Beatles Anthology*, it is the one that most musicians

I have worked with mention. They were *The Band* and Levon was a beautiful guy. That night, I raised a glass to that famous chandeliered ceiling of the Fillmore and had a drink to his memory.

NOT A SECOND TIME?

The new millennium got off to a great start when I heard the news that the Jimi Hendrix Band of Gypsys documentary had been nominated for a Grammy. We were up against documentaries on U2 and Radiohead who at that time were the two biggest bands in the world so I didn't hold out much hope of us winning this time around (unlike back in 1997 when, as I later found out, the Beatles had almost been a 'shoo-in' to win). Still, it was great to be nominated.

This time, the awards were being held in Los Angeles, at the Staples Centre. John McDermott invited me, Chips and Neil over for the ceremony. As had happened three years earlier, Chips declined the invite and Neil as usual was too busy dealing with Beatles business to attend. But any excuse to go to Los Angeles and I was on my way. On 22nd February I boarded the flight along with George Scott, who had been line producer on the film.

George and I were in the limo, heading over to the Staples Centre with John McDermott and Janie Hendrix, when John asked me if I had prepared a speech for when we won. I didn't share John's confidence and told him that I hadn't but I would make something up.

"And the winner is *Jimi Hendrix Band of Gypsys*." I honestly couldn't believe it, I never in a million years thought that we would win. Once again with shaking hands, I accepted the Grammy. I didn't have a clue what to say this time; I think I just thanked John and Janie, Chips and Neil, George Scott and Eddie Kramer, and everyone else who had helped us bring the project to fruition. I looked into the audience where I could see John McDermott, who had a big smile on his face, nodding as if to say, 'I told you there was a great documentary waiting to be made.' I handed the microphone over to Janie Hendrix, who had a speech prepared and thanked God, her dad, and in particular her brother Jimi, for bringing so much great music into the world.

Winning for the Beatles was sweet but this was even sweeter because it had won against the odds and it made me think back to when I was having a panic attack in Le Parc Hotel two years earlier, doubting that I was even going to be able to make a documentary.

This time my winning did not make the local papers back in Newcastle but to me it was a much bigger story. I had proven to myself that I could do this and maybe it might put an end to those nightmares where I ended up back in the shipyards in Wallsend. I wasn't aware of it at the time but I was one of only two directors who had ever been awarded two Grammys. I had made documentaries on the 'most famous group of all time', the 'greatest guitarist of all time', the 'greatest band of all time', and my next documentary would be on probably my own favourite band of all time.

THE WHO'S NEXT

"I am not sure if I even want to do this documentary, but I have written a letter to myself to convince myself why I should do it."

Chips, Nick de Grunwald and I were sat in a room with Pete Townshend, hoping that he would give us the go-ahead to make a film about the *Who's Next* album. For me this was one of the greatest albums of all time and contained at least two of his greatest songs, *Won't Get Fooled Again* and *Behind Blue Eyes.* But Pete was undecided if he wanted to participate in the documentary, which was why he had written himself a letter outlining the reasons why he should take part.

To date, the documentaries I had made had been on people that I liked. With Townshend it was different. I *loved* the Who. I had camped in the street to buy tickets to see them play Newcastle Odeon Cinema back in 1973, and they were responsible for my first-ever trip to London, for the Charlton Festival. Not long after that, me and my mates first started thinking that playing rock and roll, rather than just listening to it, might be a possibility. In fact, I still had a poster of Townshend on my wall at home. This bloke sat in front of me had basically changed my life.

Pete went on to say, "If I do decide to do this, I want to talk about the type of microphones we used on the amps to record the guitars, and not have to do all that stuff listening to the old tapes of the album. I hate that."

I spoke up, "That all sounds great, Pete, but all that information about microphones, that's for train spotters, whereas your fans would love all that stuff of you listening to the master tapes of the album."

Pete, I was not disappointed to say, was still an angry man and that comment from me had made him pretty angry. I thought, 'Fuck, I've blown it, I've really pissed off Pete Townshend, I've seen what he does to his guitars and now he's looking at me like he wants to do the same thing to me.' The room went silent. Then Pete said, "OK then, you're right, I'll do it."

Three weeks later, I was sat in Olympic studio in Barnes, interviewing Pete's bandmate, Roger Daltrey. This guy was to my mind one of the greatest rock singers of all time. He was friendly enough but you could tell that he wouldn't take any shit from anyone and even though he wasn't a big bloke he looked like a right hard bastard. Roger told me that at one stage during the Who's career, Pete had given him the ultimatum to either stop fighting or be kicked out of the band. Being kicked out of his own band was not an option so he had learned how to calm his temper and stop using his fists to settle arguments.

As we were going through the multi-track tapes of *Behind Blue Eyes*, one of the things that Roger highlighted was that when Keith Moon played the drums he wasn't like your normal drummer who would just keep time; Keith would in fact play the vocal line of the song. When you removed all the instruments so that all you were left with was Roger's vocals and Keith's drums, sure enough, Keith would accent every word that Roger sang. Roger was laughing at the audacity of the way that Keith played; he might have been a hard nut but there was no doubting the love and affection he felt for Keith.

We headed down to the Cotswolds to interview the bass player, John Entwistle. John lived in exactly the sort of place that I imagined a rock star would live, it was like a castle. On the walls he had shields and armour and a whole load of stuffed sharks, alongside the biggest collection of bass guitars I had ever seen in my life. When we were going through the tapes of the album, John plugged in his bass and started to play along with the track *Baba O'Riley*. John's bass was the loudest thing that I had ever heard. He said to Tim Fraser, my sound recordist, who was monitoring the sound through his headphones, "How is that for level?" Tim was pinned against the wall and his headphones had been blown off his head. John then asked him, "Do you think it could do with a bit more volume?" I am not surprised that Pete Townshend suffered from hearing problems

Next up was Pete, who we were filming at Eel Pie studios on the river at Twickenham. When he turned up, he didn't seem in the best of moods. As we were halfway through listening to the multi-tracks he said to me, "I hate doing this, I don't know why I am doing it." I told Pete that if he wasn't happy we should just stop. Pete said he would give it his best shot. We continued filming but I could tell that he was becoming more miserable, and after an hour or so I told the guys to stop filming. If Pete wasn't comfortable that would come across in the documentary and it wouldn't look good. We had him again the next day; hopefully he would be in a better mood.

The following day, I was feeling nervous that Pete might not even show; it was his call and if he decided to, he could pull the plug. We had set up to listen to the demo tapes that Pete had recorded prior to recording the album, and were then hoping to interview him and have him play and discuss the writing of his songs. Luckily for me, Pete turned up at ten o'clock, as arranged. Before I had a chance to tell him what we had planned for the day, he stopped me and told me he wanted a word with me in private. I thought, 'here we go, he's going to tell me he doesn't want to do this'. We went off into a corner, Pete put his arm around me and said, "I'm sorry about yesterday, I was feeling nervous and uncomfortable, I know how much you want to make this film and how hard you are working and I love you for that, now come on, let's have a great day today."

I was choked. This was Pete Townshend, and he was apologising to me and telling me that he loved me.

Pete played us the multi-track demos that he had made prior to recording the album. He had played all the instruments and sung himself; it didn't sound like the Who but still sounded great. One of my favourite songs that Pete had demoed for *Who's Next* was *Pure and Easy*. I mentioned to him how much I loved that song but he told me that he never performed it as it hadn't featured on the finished album. He then demonstrated how he had created the synthesiser parts that had featured on *Won't Get Fooled Again* and *Baba O'Riley*. He was so enthusiastic and obviously proud about what he had been able to create with those early synths.

When Pete sat down at the piano and was discussing the writing of his songs he said, "This is one that never made it onto the album." He proceeded to play and sing *Pure and Easy*. Here I was, sat just two feet away. I was fighting back tears. I knew he was playing it specifically because I said it was one of my favourites.

Pete was brilliant that day and what he gave me was great for the documentary.

After being in the edit suite for six weeks, we sent Pete a rough cut to get his approval. He didn't go overboard with his comments, he just said that he didn't want to make any changes. That was good enough for me. If I am asked who is the rock star I have most enjoyed working with, I always say Pete Townshend. Pete didn't let me down, he was exactly how I hoped he would be; he knew that I was a fan of the band and how much he and the Who meant to me when I was growing up. Pete Townshend remains one of my greatest heroes.

LAUGHING LOU

I never took it for granted how fortunate I was to be in my position and having the opportunity to be doing a job that I loved. It would surprise me when some of the people I worked with didn't seem to appreciate how fortunate we were to be doing what we did. Maybe it was because I had seen the other side of what life had to offer. I can tell you from experience that flying halfway across the world and having to drag yourself out of bed after only four hours' sleep to spend the day filming rock stars is preferable to spending a day lying on your back breathing in toxic fumes with your head stuck inside a welding helmet.

After finishing the *Who's Next*, there was a period of eighteen months when I never stopped working. When people asked me what I did for a living, I would say that I directed music documentaries, and not feel like I was bullshitting. I made films on Pink Floyd, Genesis, Queen and Meat Loaf. All bands whose records I had in my collection, so I never had to do a great amount of research to bring me up to speed. When I had met Alan Hull from Lindisfarne during the time that I was in White Heat, he had told me to write about what I knew. I was now applying the same logic to the documentaries I was making.

I always wanted the artist that I was working with to know that I knew my stuff, and that they were in safe hands. I had the ideal calling card. Within fifteen minutes of meeting them, I would bring the conversation around to the Beatles, who every musician loved. It was a safe bet that they had seen the *Anthology*. I would drop it into the conversation that I had been series director on the *Anthology* and had won a Grammy for my work on it. I would then remark on how recording studios had changed since I was in a band back in the 1970s and early 1980s, when we would record on twenty-four track analogue, then if need be I would mention winning my second Grammy for my Hendrix documentary.

While I was giving my spiel I would catch sight of my producer Martin Smith out of the corner of my eye and he would have this look on his face as if to say, 'Bob is going to mention the Beatles, then his Grammy, then how he was in a band, and that he won a second Grammy for his Hendrix documentary'. It seemed to work, though, and by the time we got around to start filming I generally had the artist on side.

I would also then tell them, "This is your film and it will only be as good as you allow it to be. You can be as involved as you want; at the end of the day, it's your story that is being told and it is my job to tell that story as best I can." I was discovering that the best documentaries are the ones where the subject of the film has engaged with the project. If they have entered into it with the attitude that all they have to do is just turn up and do an interview then leave and never think any more of it, that rarely makes for a good film. And if I am investing six months of my life in something, I want the end result to be as good as it can be, even if the journey to get there has been a bit bumpy. That was certainly the case when Nick de Grunwald told me that he had done a deal to make a *Classic Album* film about Lou Reed's *Transformer* album.

There is a common belief that when Lou Reed was in the Velvet Underground not many people had bought their debut album but that all those who did went on to form bands of their own. That was not the case with me and White Heat. I might have claimed at one point that we had lifted the name for the band from one of their songs but that was just bullshit on my behalf as I thought we would gain some punk rock credibility from the association. I was not a fan of Lou Reed or his former band but I had seen Lou perform on the same bill as the

Who at the Charlton Festival back in 1974; not that this would be something I would be bringing up in conversation with him as I am sure that his memories of that day would not have been as happy as mine. He was probably still reeling from the dry cleaning bill, having provoked the ire of the crowd. I was hoping that in the years since then he might have mellowed a bit.

While doing my research on Lou Reed, I discovered that anyone who had ever interviewed him seemed to share the same opinion, that he could be a bit of a twat. In fact, Lou never made any secret of how much he hated journalists, and would go out of his way to make their lives difficult. Not that I would class myself as a journalist but I had a feeling that anyone asking questions and delving into his past would be thought of as such. But I was up for the challenge. Even so, as the day that I was due to fly to New York approached, I began to feel a bit nervous.

Prior to going to New York, we had approached David Bowie - who, along with Mick Ronson, had produced the *Transformer* album - to see if he would come along to the session. At first it looked like Bowie was going to be able to make it, then a family member got sick so it didn't happen. We were able to get Ken Scott, who had engineered the album. Ken agreed to attend the session where we would play back the multi-track tapes of the album. The studio we booked for the filming had been specifically requested by Lou, as this was where he did a lot of his recording. John Simmons, my regular cameraman, was travelling with me. He lit the areas that we were going to be filming with candles and it looked fantastic. We even had the in-house engineer who Lou regularly worked with set up his favourite microphone. I wanted Lou to be happy.

Lou walked into the room and he looked great. He was dressed from head to toe in black, was as skinny as a whippet, and looked super-fit. Without any hellos or introductions, he walked straight over to the chair where he was going to be interviewed and sat down. The first thing he said was, "How am I supposed to sit on this chair?"

"Any way that you feel comfortable, Lou," was all I could think to say in answer to his question.

John Simmons suggested that Lou reverse the chair and 'sit on it like Christine Keeler in that famous photograph'. For some reason, Lou took offence at this and replied, "I don't need to be told how to sit on a chair by any smart-ass cameraman."

John was one of the nicest guys you could ever wish to meet and already he was in Lou's bad books. All of this was only making me more nervous. Eventually, though, Lou found a way to sit on the chair that worked for him.

Just as I was about to ask my first question, Lou's manager came over and whispered in my ear, "Don't ask him any questions about drugs and don't mention that he once had an affair with a transvestite." Lou had been famous for singing about drugs so my questions would probably have veered into that territory but him having once had a relationship with a transvestite was not something I had thought to mention; I made a mental note of it, regardless.

Once we started filming and I began asking Lou my questions, he was great. My nerves disappeared. I began by asking about what first got him into music, then quickly moved onto his being in the Velvet Underground. This was going much better than I could ever have expected. Lou was doing impersonations of his mate Andy Warhol and how he used to bollock him for not writing enough songs. Lou was not the most modest bloke that I have ever met; in fact, he was full of praise for himself and how great the Velvet Underground were.

When I was ready to ask him about the *Transformer* album, my first question was, "How did David Bowie come to be involved in the sessions?"

Lou replied, "I don't know, you better ask David."

I explained to him that we were not going to be able to interview David so it would be great if he could give us some background as to how it came about. Lou then said, "I don't want to talk about the *Transformer* album, why don't we talk about *Metal Machine Music*? That's a much better album." Now, in doing my research, I had tried to listen to *Metal Machine Music* and it was unlistenable. There were no songs, it was all just a load of feedback and white noise; in fact, I think Lou had recorded it to piss off his record company at the time. But beside that, this film was about the *Transformer* album which, as it was turning out, Lou didn't want to talk about. We took a break and I went to have a word with his manager.

Lou's manager had a look on his face that was a mixture of fear and happiness. "This is going great, I have never heard him be so open in an interview for years, he must really like you."

"Yeah, he might really like me but he doesn't want to talk about the album that I am here to make the documentary about."

The manager suggested that we forget about the interview for now and get Lou to go through the multi-track tapes, in the hope that this would jog his memory and he would have to talk about the *Transformer* album. I thought that might work so we moved to our next set-up, in the control room, together with Ken Scott, who had engineered the album. Ken was a respected recording engineer. He had worked with the Beatles and on most of David Bowie's earlier albums. In fact, it was Bowie who had brought Ken on board to work on the *Transformer* album back in 1972.

I am not sure if Lou even recognised Ken. He didn't seem that friendly towards him and for some reason was not very happy sat at the recording console next to him. He asked if he could have a word with me.

Lou told me that he didn't want to be sat next to Ken Scott because his large head would make Lou's look small by comparison. It was not that Ken had a large head; it was just that Lou had such a tiny head, but I didn't want to mention that. It was my job to keep the artist happy as best I could. We got around the problem by positioning Lou nearest the camera and Ken a bit further away. Lou seemed happy with that seating arrangement.

After the multi-track session, we finished for the day; part of the reason being that my nerves were feeling shot.

If day one had been tough, day two was a nightmare.

We were all on edge when Lou arrived; this was the day when I had hoped that he would play sections of the songs from the album. I explained what I would like him to do; to talk us through the subject matter of the songs and then play sections on his acoustic guitar.

"Can I ask you a question?" he said.

"Sure, Lou, anything you want."

"Do you sit at home and watch the old documentaries that you have made?"

I had to be honest and say no, I didn't, to which he replied, "Well, neither do I sit around playing and talking about the songs that I wrote years ago."

"But Lou, this documentary is about those songs, and you have agreed to do this. If I had agreed to talk about documentaries I had made then I would."

Lou ended the conversation, "Well that's your problem, not mine."

I noticed that his manager had disappeared from the room.

I said to Martin Smith, "I'm really fucked here, Martin, I don't know what I'm going to do."

Martin said he'd have a word with Lou. I saw them deep in conversation, while I stood around chatting to the crew and trying to decide on my next move. Martin returned to tell me that he had explained to Lou how I was a double-Grammy-winning director, had a good handle on what I needed for the film, and that I had his best interests at heart.

One thing I hadn't done when Lou arrived was give him my Beatles-Grammy-I was in a band once-Hendrix pitch. I never had the chance as Lou had sat straight down and we had jumped in and started filming. It would appear that Martin doing the pitch on my behalf might have had the desired effect as Lou said he wanted a word with me in private.

We were stood in a corridor away from the rest of the crew. Lou said, "Look, Bob, I know these last couple of days have been difficult for you and I understand that you have to make this documentary. What can I do to make it work for you?"

I said that what I really needed was for him to talk about, and play some sections of, his songs.

"OK," Lou said, "How about I come back in tomorrow, how does that sound?"

"That would be fantastic, Lou. I just need to check with my producer that we can afford the studio and the film crew for the extra day's filming."

I had a word with Martin and he said, "No problem; if you need the extra day, you can have it."

That night, I had a celebratory drink with the crew and I thanked them for their patience over the last couple of days, telling them that, following my chat with Lou, we would get what we needed the next day.

When Lou came in the following day, he made a big show of asking me in front of all the crew, "OK, Bob, what would you like to do today?"

"It would be great, Lou, if you could chat about and play us some bits of the songs."

Lou replied, "What did I tell you yesterday? I don't sit around playing any of my old songs."

I couldn't believe it. My heart sank and I thought, 'I'm really fucked now, we've spent the extra money on the crew and the studio hire and I am still not going to get what I need.' He had really screwed me over.

But eventually I was able to get Lou to pick up his guitar and at least strum a few chords and test the microphone to see that it was working. I told him that his voice was sounding fantastic and his sound engineer also came out of the control room and into the studio to say how great his voice was sounding. Lou seemed pleased with these compliments and he played and sang two lines from *Walk On The Wild Side*. At last, it seemed like we were getting somewhere.

He would strum a couple of chords and sing a line of a song, stop and go off on a tangent, then I would coax him back to the subject of the songs. This went on for around four hours and when we finally called it a day I probably had around ten minutes of usable material.

As we were packing away our equipment, Lou stood in the centre of the room and said, "I would just like to say you guys have been a pure pleasure."

When I got the material into the edit, we must have used every second of what we had shot with Lou. My editor, Julian Caidan, worked wonders, so much so that you couldn't see the joins, and Lou came out of it looking really great. We had got that one over the line by the skin of our teeth. I used Lou telling us 'you guys have been a pure pleasure' as the last piece of audio over the end credits.

I am sure that when Lou went home to his wife at the end of the day, he was a very different character to the one that I had met, and in fact the people that knew him, who we interviewed for the documentary, all remarked on what a sweetheart he was and how he was nothing like his public persona. I wouldn't say that I would echo Lou's sentiment about it being a 'pure pleasure' but now that he is no longer with us I am so pleased that I got to meet him and spend time with him. He had a reputation for being difficult and he didn't disappoint; I turned up to film with Lou Reed and that is who I got. He had me on my toes for every minute of those three days, it almost felt like I was in the boxing ring with someone and if I had let my guard down he would have had me. But I stood toe-to-toe with him all the way and I think he respected me for that.

I would say that I was more of a fan of his coming out of the project than I was going in.

CAPTAIN FANTASTIC

When I was in the company of the artists I was working with, I never lost sight of the fact that I was there to do a job. I was always friendly with them, and hoped that they would like me, but I would never assume that any of these people thought of me as their friend, nor did I ever think of them as being mine. I would always be up for a drink at the end of a shoot but never expected that we would still be hanging out together at the end of the evening or that I would be invited over to their place for a bite to eat. I have seen it happen where people have assumed that because they have worked alongside these famous people, they are now their friends. That's a dangerous road to go down and will end in disappointment. The people that I was often friends with were those who worked for the artist; the managers or their assistants. These would often be the people that I would deal with during the making of a documentary and it was always good to have them on side.

One such person, who was involved in artist management, was Derek MacKillop, who I had first met when he was managing Lloyd Cole. Derek would eventually manage Elton John. One night, Derek and I were having a drink and I was expressing my opinion that Elton had lost a bit of the credibility he had in his early days when, aside from being recognised as a great showman, the main focus of attention was his voice and his songs. I felt that in recent years the music seemed to have taken a back seat, at least as far as the general public were concerned, and the focus was now on his place as 'national treasure'. I told Derek that what Elton needed was to do a *Classic Album* film and that this would remind people what a great singer and songwriter he was. Derek didn't totally agree with me but said that he would bear that in mind. A couple of days later, he got in touch with the office and told us that Elton was up for doing a documentary about his *Goodbye Yellow Brick Road* album.

Derek explained that Elton was about to go on tour and was rehearsing in Los Angeles, but would be able to give us a couple of hours of his time. Elton John is probably the hardest-working man in show business and was the exception to the rule that you needed a lot of time with an artist to make a good film. Any time he offered, you would take, and make it work.

I have often found that the bigger the star, the easier they are to get along with. That was certainly the case with Elton. He must have been interviewed on film a million times and he is obviously aware that anyone meeting him for the first time is going to be a bit nervous. Within a minute of shaking hands, having noticed my accent, he asked if I supported Newcastle or Sunderland. I told him in no uncertain terms that I supported Newcastle and would in fact be heading to St James' park the following weekend, once we had finished filming in LA.

After filming we had dinner with Derek, who told me, "You should be celebrating, you've just spent two hours with one of the world's biggest stars. Not only that but Elton really liked you, and if he likes you he will want to work with you again."

I could almost have run the two hours I spent with Elton without any edits and it would have made a great documentary. The editing period for a documentary such as this is around six weeks but three weeks in we pretty much had a finished film.

Derek was right and even before we had finished the edit, I was offered the chance to work with Elton again. Carlton Television had approached him with the idea of making *The Elton John Story*. Elton agreed to the documentary on the understanding that I would direct it.

One of the great things about making a documentary on someone like Elton is that there is no shortage of people who are willing to lend their voices as to why he is such a great musician and all-round great bloke. Everyone we approached agreed to be involved; from Posh and Becks to Sting, to Graham Taylor, the former Watford United manager. We even had people offering their artists to us but we were turning them down.

One person we did interview, at his home in the Hollywood hills, was Rod Stewart. While we were setting up I asked to use the toilet and when I was in there thought I might nick a book of matches as a souvenir but decided against it. As I walked out of the toilet, Rod said, "You haven't nicked anything from my toilet as a memento, have you?" That was a close shave.

Rod had a reputation as a ladies' man so I decided to let my producer Suzy Ratner interview him. He had a twinkle in his eye when he realised that Suzy was in the interview chair rather than some bloke from Newcastle who had ideas about nicking something from his toilet. It was a good move and Suzy got some great material. At one point, he was telling her how generous Elton was, especially at Christmas time. He recalled how one Christmas he had bought Elton a mini fridge that cost him £300 and Elton had bought him a Rembrandt painting.

Rod had lived up to his reputation as someone who had an eye for the girls and as a bit of a tight wad, and had confirmed Elton's reputation for his generosity.

When we returned to the UK there were a couple of additional questions I needed to ask Elton and he suggested that we went along to film him at the BBC, prior to him recording a performance for *Top of the Pops*. As we were packing away our gear and getting ready to leave, he asked what I was up to that weekend. I told him that I was heading back up to Newcastle. He said that, had I been staying in London, I could have come along to a party he was having at his place. As it turned out, this was one of Elton's famous White Parties and guaranteed to be a celebrity-packed event, more than likely attended by most of the people we had interviewed for the documentary.

When I got back home, I told Karen that I had been invited to Elton's party.

"Why didn't you go? It would have been great."

"But I wouldn't have known anyone that was there," I said.

"You would have known everyone; it would be full of celebrities."

"Yes, I would know *who they were* but I wouldn't *know* them, and what could be worse than being in a room full of famous people?"

Karen knew what I meant. That Friday night I was out with my friends on the Quayside in Newcastle.

Come Monday morning I was back on the train to London. This had now been my routine for the past ten years. Mark Knopfler from Dire Straits, in his song *Southbound Again*, mentioned that whenever he crossed the River Tyne heading south to London he was not sure if he was 'going or leaving home'. I was beginning to understand what he meant. Not that I had ever contemplated moving full-time to London; my roots were in Newcastle and I had no intention of cutting the umbilical chord that connected me to my home city. I also had the feeling that if I was to move away I would lose the essence of what made me who I was.

AND THE BROWN DIRT COWBOY

The person who probably has the best gig in all of rock and roll is Elton's song-writing partner, lyricist Bernie Taupin. Bernie is recognised by his peers in the music business, gets to enjoy all the trappings of fame, shares the song-writing royalties of all the hits he has written with Elton, and yet would not be recognised by the average bloke in the street. And he lives on a ranch in Southern California. He really is the Brown Dirt Cowboy to Elton's Captain Fantastic. And this was pretty much how we pitched the idea to Melvyn Bragg when we suggested we should do Bernie as the subject of a *South Bank Show*.

Melvyn went for the idea and we flew out to film Bernie on his ranch. Bernie elaborated on the workings of his and Elton's partnership and explained that he is not even in the room when Elton is putting the tunes to his words. He would just send Elton the words and he would either use them or he wouldn't.

Bernie gave us a set of his lyrics that we took with us to Atlanta, where we were going to be filming with Elton. The plan was that we would film Elton reviewing them, to see if they would get his seal of approval.

When we arrived at Elton's place, I was surprised to discover that he lived in a tower block. We got in the elevator and went up to his apartment on the top floor, the whole of which was his. As we walked out of the lift, it was like entering an art gallery. Elton came to meet us in his dressing gown; he must have been having a bit of a lie-in after doing a gig the night before. While the film crew were setting up in his front room, he told me to come into his kitchen as he wanted to play me something. It was the latest release by a guy called John Mayer, called *Your Body is a Wonderland*. I had never heard of the guy but Elton was raving about him and predicting great things for him. He went on to play me a number of other songs by people I had never heard of. I wasn't sure how to react; there I was in Elton's kitchen, him still in his dressing gown. I think I might have done a little dance along to some of the songs he played.

While we stood in the kitchen, I kept shouting through to Martin Smith to ask him what the time was as I wasn't wearing a watch and was aware that we only had a limited amount of time to shoot what we needed. I had heard that Elton would regularly give a gift of a watch to people who had worked with him and you can bet that it wouldn't be a Timex or a Swatch; the least you would expect would be a Rolex. Not that I was expecting a gift of a watch, I just wanted to let him know that I had my eye on the time!

We had set up to film at his piano and the plan was that we would surprise him with Bernie's lyrics. I gave these to Elton and asked if he could write a tune to them. He studied the sheet of paper for around thirty seconds, played a few notes on the piano, then said, "This would be a sort of Neil Young-type thing." He proceeded to sing. Within two minutes, he had turned Bernie's lyrics into a song. If I hadn't been in the room, I wouldn't have believed it.

At the end he laughed and said, "Sorry, Bernie, that one doesn't work for me."

When I was editing the programme, after hearing the song a couple of times, I couldn't get it out of my head. It made me wonder how many great songs those two have written which never made it onto tape, let alone a record.

The section we filmed in Atlanta was one of the highlights of the *South Bank Show* and I was explaining this to Derek when I went to visit him one Friday morning at the offices of Elton's management company, Rocket, prior to catching the train home to Newcastle. Derek said that Elton happened to be playing at the Arena in Newcastle that night; he suggested that I go along and that Elton would be really pleased to see me. He said I could take a couple of my mates and should go backstage before the show as Elton would be flying back to London as soon as it was over.

I got back to Newcastle and asked two of my mates, Tony Boot and Gav, if they fancied coming along to the gig. I am not sure they were that keen at first but once I said we had backstage passes and would get to meet Elton it became a good idea.

We turned up at the arena and were escorted to Elton's dressing room. We stood outside for a couple of minutes then one of his guys told us that he would see us. The room looked nothing like the dressing rooms I had frequented in the past. There was no array of booze and cold sandwiches; it had been customised with low lighting, comfortable sofas, and enough flowers to open a florist's shop. Elton was sat on a sofa, wearing a short kimono-style dressing gown. He got up and greeted me with a hug, and I introduced him to Tony and Gav. He shook hands with them and then sat back down. We chatted about my plans for the weekend, and my return to London to continue the edit on the *South Bank Show*. Tony and Gav never spoke a word. I hadn't known either of them to be so quiet in all my life. They just sat and stared at Elton.

We were only in there around fifteen minutes as Elton was due on stage. I wished him good luck for the gig and said I hoped to see him again soon.

We took our seats in the arena. It was a great show. Halfway through, Elton said, "It's great to be here in Newcastle and I would like to dedicate this song to two of my friends who are here tonight: the manager of Newcastle United, Bobby Robson, and my friend Bob Smeaton." He played his most recent hit, *I Want Love*. It was a great moment and even got a mention in the review of the gig the following night in the *Evening Chronicle*.

As we were leaving the arena, I asked Tony and Gav why they had not said anything to Elton. Gav said he was scared to take his eyes off

Elton's face, in case he might have forgotten to put his underpants on. Elton is 'rock royalty' and Gav said he was worried he might catch a glimpse of the 'crown jewels'.

THE BEST JOB I NEVER HAD

I had now made three documentaries with Elton and had the feeling that I had gained his trust. I started thinking about another project. Having witnessed the way that Elton and Bernie worked, Martin Smith and I thought it might be an idea to suggest to Derek that the next time he was due to record an album, we film Elton writing the melodies to Bernie's lyrics, then follow the process through and observe how the meat is put on the bones of the songs.

We knew it wouldn't be workable to have a film crew hanging around the recording studio all hours of the day and suggested that we could have rigged cameras that wouldn't need to be manned but could be set to film the whole time that Elton was in the studio. It would almost be like Elton and his band were contestants in the television series *Big Brother*, which had just started in the UK. We would be filming every moment that they were there, capture the highs and lows of them recording, and hopefully be on hand for the creation of another *Your Song* or *Candle in the Wind*. Derek put this idea to Elton, who was up for it. We had to pack our bags as Elton and his band were due to start recording in LA in a couple of weeks.

Martin and I checked into the Mondrian Hotel, which would be our base for the three weeks that Elton had set aside to record his album. The Mondrian was, at the time, probably the hippest hotel in West Hollywood. The hotel's bar, the Sky Bar, was fantastic and had an amazing view of the city which at night would be lit up by a million twinkling lights. Jim Morrison wasn't wrong when he called LA 'the city of lights', and the bar around the pool was a great place to enjoy that view.

Come the weekend, the Sky Bar was the place to be seen. To gain entrance, you had to be a celebrity, really good looking, or a resident of the hotel. Martin and I both fell into the latter category or we would have never have made it past the doorman.

On the morning that we were due to start filming, Derek called and asked Martin and me if we could come to the Beverly Hills Hotel for a breakfast meeting. When we got there he told us that Elton had decided that he wasn't in the right frame of mind to start recording a new record and had sent the producer and all the band members home on the understanding that they would reconvene at a later date. Martin and I were gutted. We had been looking forward to getting started and now we were looking at a twelve-hour flight home with nothing to show for our efforts. Derek told us, "Look, why don't you stay over for a week at the hotel and have a bit of a holiday? We will pick up the tab. I know how disappointed you are that this isn't going ahead at present, and the amount of work that has already gone into it, so we will pay you for the job regardless."

Thanks, Elton. If you ever need someone not to make a documentary about you, I'm your man.

It was eight years before I saw Elton again; I was making another documentary and I had requested that he contribute to it. He was as busy as ever but said that he could give me ten minutes of his time before he was due to go on stage for a concert he was giving at Hatfield House in Hertfordshire.

We set up the camera in a tiny room backstage. Elton came in, sat down, and talked non-stop for ten minutes. As usual, everything that he gave us could have been included in the doc. When we finished the interview, he was getting up to leave and said, "Bob, I thought I recognised your voice. I couldn't see your face because of the light that was set up behind your head." He took me to meet his baby son Zachary, who must have only been about six months old. Elton was a really proud dad. He told me it was great to catch up again, shook my hand, then he walked on stage to perform in front of 20,000 people. I have nothing but praise for him; he is a total professional and a great bloke, and I was privileged to have spent time in his company.

THE ONES THAT GOT AWAY

While I was hanging out in LA, courtesy of Elton and his management, I got a call from the office in London to ask if I would be up for a trip to San Francisco, to have a meeting with Carlos Santana, who had expressed an interest in having a documentary made about him. Carlos had recently had a resurgence in popularity and had pretty much cleaned up at the 2000 Grammy Awards when he picked up eight awards following the release of his most recent album, *Supernatural*. The timing seemed right; all we had to do was convince the man himself. Nick de Grunwald felt that if I went along and met him it would possibly seal the deal.

I caught the short flight from LA to San Francisco and jumped in a cab to take me to the office of Carlos Santana. When I arrived, I had a feeling that the cab driver had brought me to the wrong place. The office was situated on an industrial estate on the outskirts of the city. It looked just like Team Valley back home in Newcastle and not really the sort of place where you would expect a multiple-Grammy-winner to be situated.

I asked the cab driver if he could wait for me while I checked if this was the place I was meant to be then I walked into an office that looked like the reception for a used car salesroom. However, there were a couple of gold discs on the wall so I guessed I was at the right place. I told the lady on reception that I had come to see Carlos Santana and that he was expecting me. I sat there for a couple of minutes then a guy came in and asked me if I was here to see Carlos Santana. I told him that I was. He looked a lot like Carlos and I thought maybe it was his brother. The guy then left the reception. I sat there for another five minutes before the receptionist said, "You can go through now."

I walked into the office and sitting behind the desk was the same guy I had seen five minutes earlier. Maybe this was actually Carlos Santana. He said to me, "I hear you want to do a documentary about Carlos Santana." I told him that was true. He explained to me that if Carlos agreed to do a documentary it should be called *Phenomenon*, as that's what Carlos was. I agreed that was a great title, and that in fact we could even call the documentary *Carlos Santana, Phenomenal Genius*. The guy gave me a strange look and said, "No, just *Phenomenon* will do."

I chatted a bit longer and told him our idea for the documentary was to make something along the lines of a Carlos Santana's greatest hits *Classic Album*. I wasn't convinced he liked the idea; the expression on his face wasn't giving anything away. I was doing most of the talking and had pretty much run out of things to say so told him it was great to meet him and that I had a flight to catch back to LA. We shook hands and I left the office feeling really confused; I was not sure if I had met Carlos Santana, his brother, or just a bloke that looked like him. As I left the office, the receptionist said, "Thanks for coming in, Carlos will be in touch."

The cab driver was still sat waiting for me outside and asked me if this was the right address, and did I get to meet Carlos Santana? I told him I wasn't sure. On my way back to the airport, I rang the office in London. They asked me how the meeting had gone. I said I thought it had gone well, but wasn't sure who it had been with. One thing was certain; if we did get to make the documentary, we had a great title for it.

As it turned out, we never did get to make the documentary; someone from Carlos' office got in touch to say that he didn't feel the time was right.

Just recently I was watching a documentary about Miles Davis where Carlos Santana was being interviewed. During the interview he made a derogatory comment about people who had criticised Miles' music and the end of his comment he said, "Damn it Carlos, that is harsh."

At that moment I knew that it was Carlos that I had met in that office in San Francisco. It would appear that when you are a phenomenon it's OK to talk about yourself in the third person!

Another one that got away was Van Morrison. I had long been a fan of Van and thought that I had got on reasonably well with him when he had featured in the *Danny Boy* film. I had also heard from Jools Holland that he had recently bumped into Van, who had told him that he was thinking about doing a documentary about his life and that he was going to get Bob Smeaton to direct it. I passed this information on to Julian Lloyd, whose idea it had been to make the *Danny Boy* film, and suggested he get in touch with Van. Maybe we could meet up to have a chat about doing a documentary on his life. We also contacted Melvyn Bragg and asked if he would be up for featuring Van as the subject of a *South Bank Show*. Melvyn said yes straight away. By all accounts, they had been chasing Van for years but had always been turned down.

Julian, Chips Chipperfield and I went along to meet Van, prior to him playing a gig in Nottingham. We sat down and had a cup of tea with him while he ate a bowl of custard. We explained that Melvyn Bragg was keen to do a documentary on Van's life, and that the *South Bank Show* would finance this. Van told us that he didn't need Melvyn Bragg's money and that he would finance it himself. He went on to say that he didn't enjoy being interviewed on camera. I told Van, "That's not a problem, there will be no cameras involved when I interview you." My plan was to sit down and record an interview with him on audio tape only; we could use his voice to narrate his story. The only time we would see Van would be on archive footage. He really went for this idea; we shook hands and agreed to speak again over the next couple of days. We watched Van do his gig; he was brilliant and hadn't even changed his shirt or tie from when we'd spoken. When you are Van the Man, you don't have to worry about things like stage outfits.

The afternoon after our meeting, Chips got a call from 'Van's man', who told him that Van had requested that we travel down to meet him the following day at his place in Bath, to talk further about the documentary. At the time that Chips took the call, he had returned home to his place in Dingle over in Ireland. He explained that he would need a couple of days to make plans, then he would travel to Bath and we could continue our discussion. Chips was told, "Van wants to see you tomorrow or it's off." When Chips broke this news to me I said, "Come on, this is a great chance. Van's a legend, we have him on side, and he is going to finance it."

Chips told me, "Bob, if I jump on a plane and meet Van tomorrow, he will think he has us at his beck and call and will start ordering us around, and then we will be fucked."

I agreed with what Chips was saying, even though I would have been on the train to Bath in a heartbeat. But Chips was one of my best mates and I respected him and the point he was making, and maybe he was right.

We never heard another word from Van Morrison. That meeting we had in Nottingham was eighteen years ago and to this day there is still no sign of the elusive Van Morrison documentary. But he is Van and he is 'the Man' and he will have the documentary made one day, and you can bet it will be on his terms.

I SHALL BE RELEASED

Have you ever heard of something called the Festival Express?

When John McDermott asked me that question during the summer of 1999, I had no idea what he was talking about. John suggested I call Eddie Kramer, who would be able to shed some light on it. I did just that and Kramer told me that he had met a guy called Garth Douglas, who had access to film footage shot at a series of music festivals that had taken place across Canada back in 1970. I contacted Garth, who explained to me that he had found this film footage in the Canadian national film archive. He also told me that the groups had travelled between the festivals on a private train, and that this had also been filmed. The train and subsequent festivals were all part of the Festival Express.

I flew up to Canada to meet Garth, who at the time was working with a guy called James Cullingham. They were hoping to do something with the footage that had been found. I looked at some; it was fantastic. Among the many artists who were captured on film were the Grateful Dead, the Band, Janis Joplin, and Buddy Guy. I asked Garth what the audio was like. He explained that the festivals had been recorded on eight-track, so the audio would be great. The only problem was that none of the artists who were involved had signed any release forms so that pretty much meant none of the film or sound material could be used. Without the artists' signatures, it was a no-go. It looked like Festival Express would be another one that got away.

Six months later, I got a call from Gavin Poolman, whose father Willem had been the producer of what he intended to be a film of the Festival Express. Back in 1970 Willem had hoped that this proposed film would follow on from the likes of *Monterey Pop* and *Woodstock*, which had shown that there was an appetite for festival films. *Festival Express* would have the added ingredient of the bands travelling by train.

Because of financial and contractual problems, the film was never completed. The project pretty much fell apart. Willem had lost their house because of his investment in *Festival Express*. Gavin, however, was nothing if not confident and told me that we were going to finish off what his father had started. We were going to make this film. He was aware that there were no agreements with any of the artists, and that to get their signatures retrospectively and to make this film would cost millions of pounds. He asked me if I would cut a taster to show to potential investors. I had nothing to lose; it was a long shot but there was a chance this could lead to me directing my first feature film.

We approached Eddie Kramer and asked him if he would mix three songs; one from each of the three biggest names that we wanted to include in the taster: the Grateful Dead, the Band, and Janis Joplin. Kramer agreed, on the understanding that if we were able to raise the money to make the film, he would get to mix the soundtrack. He sent me mixes of the three songs we had requested for inclusion in the trailer. They sounded brilliant.

My old pal Chips Chipperfield put me in touch with an editor in Dublin called Eamonn Power, who he suggested could possibly work with me on putting the trailer together. I met with Eamonn and not only was he one of the funniest and nicest guys that I had ever met, he did a fantastic job cutting the trailer. When we showed it to Gavin, he danced around the edit suite with tears in his eyes and told us, "This is better than I could ever have imagined, we are going to make this film and it will get its world premiere at the Toronto Film Festival next year, and my dad will be in the audience to watch his dream come to fruition."

Six months after he had danced around the room of the edit suite in Dublin, Gavin broke the news to me that he, along with his business partner John Trapman, had shown the trailer to some rich friends of theirs who were massive music fans and were prepared to put up the vast majority of the money needed to finance the film. There was one proviso; we could only access the funds if Janis Joplin, the Grateful Dead and the Band all agreed to feature in the film. We were in a Catch 22 situation. None of those artists would agree to let us feature them until they saw the finished film, and we couldn't start to make the film until they had agreed to being part of it. As I mentioned earlier, Gavin Poolman was a very confident young man. He told me, "Bob, you will make a great film. Why would they not want to be part of it? Let's start spending the money and make this film."

I knew that in order to get the artists to agree to be in the film, the first thing they would consider was how good their musical performances were. They were not going to have a problem with how they looked; these artists were all in their prime and looked fantastic back in 1970. Before I even began looking at the film footage, I put together what I thought would be the soundtrack and made my choices as to what would feature in the film, based on the best-sounding on-stage performances. I then started to find the pictures that went with the audio.

Originally, I didn't want to shoot any additional material but as we worked through what we had I realised that the footage was not providing enough narrative as to what we were watching. I decided to go ahead and interview a number of those artists who had been part of the whole experience and those fans who had attended the festivals.

The first musicians that I interviewed about their memories of Festival Express were the surviving members of the Grateful Dead. They all agreed it was a great time and they had nothing but happy memories of that train ride across Canada. When I was interviewing Phil Lesh, he asked me what we were going to use as visuals for the film. It appeared that none of the guys in the Dead had any recollection that there were cameras filming them, on the train or at the concerts. As was the spirit of the day, and as I had witnessed in the film footage, there were a lot of drugs being consumed and I imagined that the last thing they were thinking about was that guy pointing a camera at them. All of the surviving members of the Dead agreed that we could feature them in the film as long as they *didn't* get top billing.

I then interviewed a guy called Ken Walker, who was a concert promoter, and whose idea it was to stage the Festival Express. The character I interviewed appeared physically not to have changed much from the one I had viewed on archive. This was despite the fact that, a number of years after the Festival Express had rolled over Canada, Ken had put a gun in his mouth and pulled the trigger. He must have been feeling pretty bad when he put that gun in his mouth, but he must have felt a whole lot worse when he awoke from a coma a month later. The bullet had blown the top of his skull off and although, amazingly, it didn't kill him, it did damage the right side of his brain, and left him with a hole in his head. When I interviewed him, he showed me the dent where the bullet had exited his skull.

Ken was delighted that we were making the film. Gavin was really pleased that the film had his blessing and promised him that he would have a front-row seat when the film premiered at the Toronto film festival.

In June of 2003, four years after I had my first conversations with Gavin, Eamonn and I had a cut of the film that we were happy with. Gavin then had to get the all-important remaining clearances to allow us to release the film. The first people we showed it to were the Janis Joplin estate. Janis was fantastic in the movie and those who had seen her performance said it was one of the greatest of hers ever captured on film. We knew the estate couldn't do anything but agree to let us use Janis in the film, which they did.

The Band had famously not allowed themselves to be included in the *Woodstock* film, which is probably the most famous festival film of all time, so we were really nervous that they wouldn't sign. Robbie Robertson was the second to last person to do so and I like to think that it helped that he knew me from when I made the Band's *Classic Album* film.

The last person to agree was Levon Helm. Gavin was going to head out to Woodstock to meet with him. Before he left, I told him not to mention that it was me that had made the *Classic Album* film, as I was aware that he was not a fan of that documentary. Gavin sat down with Levon and over a big fat spliff and a glass of whiskey, Levon agreed that the Band should be in the film. We had all the relevant signatures needed.

Gavin and John Trapman broke the news to the investors. They were overjoyed that we could now get started on assembling the film and asked how long it would be before they could see a cut of the film. Gavin told them we had already finished it.

Thirty-three years after the cameras had first rolled on Festival Express, the movie received its world premiere at the Toronto International Film Festival. Gav had been good to his word and we had finished what his dad had started, and *Festival Express* had finally reached its intended destination, on the big screen.

Sat in the front row was Ken Walker, grinning from ear to ear. Halfway through the film, he turned to me, gave me the thumbs-up and mouthed the words 'mazel tov'. Sat alongside Ken were Willem and Gavin Poolman. Seeing Gav and his dad sat together brought a lump to my throat.

Earlier that year, when we were almost at the end of the edit, I had received a call from my sister Suzanne. She told me that my dad was really ill with cancer and she didn't think he had long to live. I told her to ask him if he wanted me to come up to Scotland and see him. I didn't want to just turn up, as I wasn't sure if he was still denying to his wife that I was his son, and I didn't want to blow the secret that he had kept for so long. He told our Sue that he didn't want me to visit him. Four weeks later, he died.

I had mixed feelings. The sadness that I felt was that, because of some stupid lies he told in denying that I was his son, I was not able to have any sort of relationship with him between my late teens up to the day he died. One thing that was undeniable was the massive influence he had on me and how much he had shaped the person that I had become.

I have tried to take what I thought were negatives and turn these into positives. Had he tried to talk me out of following the path that he had travelled, in becoming a welder in the shipyards, I might have ended up in a job that I liked, and not been so desperate to get out of there and make something more of my life. He would tell me that I would never amount to anything, but this only served to put fuel in my tank, and drove me forward in my efforts to prove that I would amount to something.

Because I never really had any sort of relationship with him this might be the reason why Brian Mawson, Geoff Wonfor and Chips Chipperfield would become so important in my life. I wouldn't go as far as to say they were father figures but they were all older than me and I would often turn to them for advice and support.

I didn't attend my dad's funeral for the same reason I didn't go to see him when he was sick; I didn't want to blow his cover. When our Suzanne was at his funeral she approached his wife and said, "I have something to tell you."

Before Sue could say any more, my dad's wife stopped her and said, "I know what you are going to say, you have a brother called Bob, and Bob was his dad."

My sister asked her how she knew.

"It was obvious he was his son; any time his name would appear on television, he would have this big look of pride of his face."

I no longer hate him like I did when I was growing up but I am still angry at the way he treated my mam. She deserved better and she never did have another relationship after they broke up when she was only 50. I have spoken to her about him on many occasions. She recently told me that he was the only man that she had ever slept with and that she still loves him.

MIAMI

I had made my first feature film and I thought that would be it for me as far as *Festival Express* was concerned. Then we started getting requests to show the film at various film festivals around the world. The deal was that I would fly into the city where the festival was being held and be put up in a hotel for a couple of days. I would do press and publicity and then attend the screening of the film in a local cinema. After the film was shown, there would be a question-and-answer session with the audience, who would ask questions as to how the film came to be made and what my favourite part of it was. I would then head off to the bar, where the people who had not asked questions in the cinema would engage me in conversation which, more often than not, would be as much about the Beatles as it was about *Festival Express*.

The winter of 2004 was brutal so when the offer came to head out to Florida to show the film at the Miami Film Festival, and potentially grab a bit of winter sunshine, I agreed to go along.

Ten hours after leaving the UK, I arrived blinking into the Miami sunshine and was picked up by a representative of the festival, who drove me to my hotel. I got into my room, opened the curtains and looked out over Miami Beach and the sunshine sparkling on the Atlantic Ocean. I called back home to tell Karen that I had arrived 'safe and sound'. She told me that it was snowing back in Newcastle.

We screened the film and the audience loved it. The Q&A session afterwards went really well and then it was off to a party that was being held in the rooftop bar of one of the hotels on Miami Beach. I met a young woman who worked for the film festival and I spent most of my time hanging out with her. I told her that I was in a relationship back in the UK, so we knew nothing could come of us spending time together, but we enjoyed each other's company. I was meant to be in Miami for five days. I ended up staying for two weeks.

Within a week of returning to Newcastle, I was back in America, as the film was being screened at film festivals in New York, New Mexico, San Francisco and Bermuda. When we showed *Festival Express* in San Francisco, all the surviving members of the Grateful Dead turned up for the screening and at the party afterwards I got up on stage and sang with the band. I was having the best time ever; it was like being on the road with a band but the film would do the gig and then I would get to hang out with the audience and have a bit of a party afterwards, before driving or flying to the next city. I had been working solidly for eight years and this felt like the first time that I wasn't worrying about when the next job was going to start. I was out there promoting my first feature film and I was away from home for two months; the longest time that I had ever spent away from Newcastle.

But if the truth be told, my friend that I had met in Miami had also been on the road with me. My head had been turned, and over the next six months, given the slightest excuse, I would be back on the plane to Miami, where my new friend lived. She was almost twenty years younger than me and I was displaying all of the traits of a midlife crisis. But, rather than hit the drink and the drugs, I did the opposite. She didn't do either and I joined her in abstaining, adopting a healthy lifestyle. I had never felt better in my life.

That December, I celebrated my birthday in Miami. Some people that I had met while I was there were having a party at their house and invited me along. It turned out that one of the hosts was involved in cosmetic surgery and the event was in fact a 'Botox party'. It was the first time that I had ever attended a party where Botox was on the menu. After a few drinks, a number of the guests had Botox injections, and it didn't look too bad. The woman who was doing the injecting knew that it was my birthday and said that she would give me a few shots as a present. I thought, 'if you can't beat 'em, join 'em', so I had a few shots in my forehead. She probably wished she hadn't made the offer; she obviously hadn't noted the size of my forehead.

The next morning, when I woke up, I looked in the mirror. I looked ten years younger and I thought to myself, 'it's Botox for me from now on'. But the following day when I caught sight of my reflection, I nearly passed out. I had a full-on Elvis sneer going on. It looked like I was paralysed down one side of my face. I rang the woman who had given me the injections and she told me I was experiencing what is known as a 'trickle down', when the Botox trickles down the side of your face and freezes part of your lip. I was told not to worry as it would eventually wear off and my face would return to normal. That was a relief as I was flying back to Newcastle a week later. She then broke the news that it would take around two months for it to wear off. It was the worst birthday present I had ever had.

When I arrived back in Newcastle for Christmas, I was scared to smile as, when I did, part of my face didn't move. I told Karen what I had done and she gave me a right bollocking. No one else noticed but when I visited my mam, she started crying; she was convinced that I had had a stroke.

I told her what I had done and she too went crazy with me and told me that I was an idiot and that I had 'broken my smile'.

COME AS YOU ARE

Two weeks into the new year, my face was just about back to normal. I was on a flight back to America, to film material for a *Classic Album* documentary about Nirvana's *Nevermind*. Prior to starting filming, I called around to see my niece, Alba, who was seventeen at the time and a fan of the band. She had posters of Kurt Cobain on her wall and would often wear a t-shirt that was adorned with the distorted smiley face that was the Nirvana logo. I asked what it was that made Nirvana great. She said they had great songs but a lot of it was to do with Kurt and the way he spoke to his audience, and the way that they related to him. She went on to tell me that I wouldn't get that connection as I was too old. She told me not to worry too much about that, though, as she was sure that I would still make a good documentary. This made me realise that for the first time I was making a film about a band or an artist younger than me. It was a sign of the times.

The first location that we had planned to film at in America was Aberdeen, where Kurt Cobain was born, just over 100 miles from Seattle. By all accounts, it was a really desolate and depressing place and, according to the legend, it was growing up here that shaped the young Kurt and not only gave him the motivation to move to Seattle but also the inspiration for a couple of the songs that ended up on *Nevermind*. The song *Something in the Way* was written partly in reference to the time when things got so bad at home that he slept under a bridge that crossed the Wishkah river that runs through Aberdeen.

At first I thought we must have come to the wrong place. Aberdeen was surrounded by mountains and forests; all the houses had gardens out front and in the gardens were children's swings and bicycles. The bridge that Kurt had slept under crossed a river that had fish in it. This place was idyllic compared to Benwell; it felt and looked middle class. I could only imagine that when Kurt was living there it was a lot worse. Luckily for us, it started raining so that when we filmed we were able to make the place look a bit miserable.

When I interviewed Dave Grohl, he was at a loss as to why we were interested in making a documentary about Nirvana. It was as though he hadn't realised the impact that they had upon the world, or maybe he was just being modest. When he found out that I had worked with the Beatles, he said that whenever people mentioned him and his drumming, they always mentioned John Bonham from Led Zeppelin when in fact he was also a massive fan of Ringo and said that a lot of people underestimated what a great drummer Ringo was. We were ten minutes into the interview and he was still talking about Ringo's hi-hat technique. I had to remind him that we were there to talk about Nirvana.

While we were listening to the multi-track tapes of the album with the record's producer, Butch Vig, there was a moment when he soloed Kurt's voice during *Smells Like Teen Spirit*. It sounded fantastic. Butch explained that Kurt didn't like double-tracking his vocals in the studio and the only way that he could get him to do the double tracking was to tell him that was how John Lennon used to record his vocals. I couldn't believe the number of times that John and the Beatles were mentioned during the time that we were filming.

By the time we had finished, I had gained a better insight into what made Nirvana great. Alba had pointed me in the right direction and she was right; they were not a band that spoke for my generation. But there was a connection I felt between Kurt Cobain and the likes of Elvis Presley, John Lennon, Jimi Hendrix, Bob Marley, and Joe Strummer, aside from the fact that they were all originals and had all died way too young. They had each spoken for a specific generation but would also find a connection with future generations because the music they left behind was timeless.

The filming had taken around three weeks. We had travelled to Los Angeles, New York and Seattle. We hadn't done any filming in Miami but that was where I ended up for two weeks once the shoot was over.

INDOOR FIREWORKS

When I got back to Newcastle after being in America for five weeks, Karen sat me down and asked me what was going on. She said she couldn't understand the way I was behaving. She correctly pointed out that I seemed to be constantly on edge while I was home and she also remarked on the fact I had lost a load of weight. I had in fact lost over a stone because of my new healthy lifestyle, and because of the stress of what amounted to living two lives. And even though we could now laugh about the whole Botox experience, it was very unlike me to do something like that. She asked me if I was seeing someone else in America and if that was the reason I kept flying back and forth. I had to come clean. Karen told me I had to decide: did I want to be in Newcastle with her, or I did I want to be in Miami? I told her I wanted to make a go of it in America. She said if that's what I wanted to do then I should go ahead and do it.

On 4ᵗʰ July 2005, I left the UK with a heavy heart because of the pain that I had caused Karen but since I had come clean about what had been going on I also felt that a weight had been lifted from my shoulders and I was excited at the prospect of living in America.

I signed up with the William Morris agency, who said they would be able to get me film work and that I should be looking to move outside of doing documentaries and towards doing drama. This all sounded great; those Americans had a way of saying things that made you believe you could do anything. But before I could be employed in America, I would have to get a green card that would give me authorisation to live and work there. I went to see an immigration lawyer and was told that because I had won two Grammys, I would qualify as what is known as a 'desirable alien' and that I shouldn't have any trouble being granted a green card.

The agent at William Morris was good to her word and two weeks later a feature film script dropped through my letter box in Miami. The script was for a film called *Chapter 27* and was about Mark Chapman, the guy who murdered John Lennon. The first thing I did after I had read the script was get in touch with Apple to tell them that I was in the frame to make this film. I then told them I had no intention of even meeting the producers of the film. The Beatles trusted me and had been very loyal to me, and that stood for a great deal in both their eyes and mine.

I got back in touch with the woman at William Morris and thanked her for sending me the script then told her that I didn't want to meet the producers and that I would not go near any film about the guy who murdered John Lennon. The film did get made a number of years later and Jared Leto played the role of Mark Chapman. I cannot tell you if it was good or bad as I have never watched it.

I was also in discussion with John McDermott at Experience Hendrix, about making a feature-length documentary that would cover Jimi's life, from birth to death. The plan was that the documentary would be my first job that would be filmed and edited wholly in America; we were hoping to start production once my green card was sorted. Everything was falling into place. My new friend and I were getting along great and I loved being in Miami; I couldn't believe that I was living in a place where palm trees grew. I was up early every morning and running on the beach. It seemed perfect.

But I wanted to go home. I had not totally cut my ties with Newcastle and as great as Miami was, something didn't feel right. It didn't feel like home; it was almost like I was living in a dream which I knew I was going to wake up from pretty soon. I told my friend how I felt and she told me that I had to sort myself out as this had been going on for two years and I had to decide whether I wanted to 'fish or cut bait'. I was unable to make a decision and she said that if that was the case, she would make it for me. She told me this was no longer working for her.

I think that part of the reason that I was not able to make a clean break was because I hated the fact that I was repeating the pattern of what my dad had done with my mam; constantly coming and going and saying that he was going to make it work this time. I was doing the same thing with Karen and my friend, and they both deserved better.

Not long after my return to Newcastle, Ray Laidlaw (the drummer in Lindisfarne) asked if I would be up for singing at a tribute concert that was being given in memory of his band mate Alan Hull who had died nine years earlier. Alan was a great guy and had always been there to offer words of wisdom when I had been in a band. To be asked to be part of the event was a privilege and I jumped at the chance.

The concert was held at Newcastle City Hall on 20th November 2006. Geoff Wonfor was also there to film the concert for DVD release and it was great to catch up with him again. I got up and sang the Lindisfarne song *Caught in the Act* and then as the final song of the evening I joined the other performers for a rousing version of *Run for Home*. I looked out into the crowd as over two thousand Geordie voices rang out as one during the chorus. That evening that song took on a whole new meaning for me.

At the time I did feel happy to be home but there is a part of me that will always wonder how differently things might have played out had I made more of a go of it in America. Karen and I tried to patch things up but our relationship was never the same and we did eventually break up but we remain good friends.

Playing an inflatable Telecaster for Big Al Peacock and Nigel Steel.

Warming up for a night on the Quayside with John Porteous,
Tony Boot and Gav Kirkup.

Filming Classic Albums with the Who's Roger Daltrey.

Martin Smith, Dave Grohl and me filming the *Nevermind* Classic Album.

Bootsy Collins in Miami dressed for a day in the studio.

The top of the mountain in Rio.

With Mick Attridge, my mate from the Shipyards.
Bondi Beach, 2017.

With my best friend Archie in Sydney January 2018.

THE TIMES THEY ARE A CHANGIN'

LET'S HEAR IT FOR THE GIRLS

During spring 2007, I got a call from Bob Massie who had produced the documentary that I had made on Queen a number of years earlier. Bob told me that there was a big documentary being proposed, which he thought I might be interested in. I asked him who it was about and he said he wasn't at liberty to tell me but that they were a group who had split up seven years previously and were getting back together for a reunion tour. I asked him to give me more information. He told me that they were one of the biggest bands ever but I still didn't have much idea as to who they might be. Then he mentioned in passing that they were an all-girl band. I guessed the name of the group but Bob told me I couldn't mention it to anyone, it was top secret.

Two weeks later, I was sat in the office of the guy who managed the group. He explained that he had already met with a number of directors, who had put forward their ideas as to how they would make the documentary. Martin Smith was sat in on the meeting with me. I could tell by the look on his face that he was wondering how I was going to play this. It was one occasion where to go into my usual spiel re: *The Beatles Anthology* would not have worked. None of this band were even born when the Beatles were changing the world. But I knew that their manager was a massive Beatles fan and that he would have the final say as to who was going to direct the documentary.

The first question the manager asked me was who I would use to narrate the documentary and who, aside from the girls, I would want to interview. I told him that this was their story and they should tell it; people wanted to hear their version, not a scripted one. Therefore, it wouldn't need a voice-over. And I didn't feel that we would need any contributors, aside from the girls themselves. I am not sure if he was totally sold on that idea.

Then I dropped into the conversation that when we had made *The Beatles Anthology*, we hadn't used a voice-over, as people wanted to hear the Beatles themselves tell their story, and the same thing would apply here. Just before I got up to leave, I told him his group had a massive influence on fashion and on popular culture, and therefore deserved to be given the same respect and the same treatment that we had given the Beatles when we made the *Anthology*. I didn't go as far as to say that their songs were as good.

Two days later, I got the call to say that I had the gig. When I signed my contract to make the film, for the first time ever I also had to sign a non-disclosure agreement, which stated that I was not allowed to disclose the name of the group that I was working with.

I had done the band that were the first and biggest boy band and, thanks to my association with them, I was now about to do the world's biggest ever girl band. I did have a brief moment when I wondered what making this would do for my credibility; it was totally unlike anything I had done before and one thing was certain, I never had any of their records in my collection. The approach that I was going to take to making this was to show that, whether you loved them or hated them, there could be no denying the impact they had on the world during the period 1996-2000.

The idea was that I would interview the girls at the start of the process of them getting back together, then there would be a hiatus of three months while one of the girls, who was pregnant, had her baby.

The first round of interviews went really well; they were all very honest and open about each other and the effect that the level of fame they had achieved had on their lives, and the reasons why they had broken up. There were a lot of tears and, it would appear, a number of scores to settle. The plan was that I would catch up with them later in the year to interview them again, to film the rehearsals and build-up to the start of the tour.

At the end of October, I got the call to say that the girls were about to begin rehearsals for the tour and that these would be happening in Los Angeles. They had chosen LA for their base, I imagined, because this was where two of the girls were living. I was told to fly over to film and to do my second round of interviews. I must admit, I thought they were cutting it a bit fine, expecting to have a show of the scale that they were proposing up and ready to go in just over a month. One of the choreographers who was working with them told me that a show of this scale would normally take at least three months of rehearsals and you had to take into account that they had not performed on stage together in over nine years. As we watched them rehearse, I had my doubts that they would be ready for the first show in Vancouver on 2nd December.

Having done the second round of interviews, a couple of the girls approached me and asked that I not use certain things they had said in the first interview they had given back in July. I explained that I had already started assembling the documentary and that what they had said four months ago was still relevant now; these interviews would show the process of how, during the build-up to the concerts, they had become best friends again, and that this was all part of the healing process. The gigs would be proof of that.

I won my argument and they agreed to let me leave in the quotes that I had used. Then one of the girls told me that I couldn't use *any* of her first interview. I asked why not and she explained that since that interview she had changed her hair from blonde to black and that it would look strange in the documentary. I pointed out that the audience would be aware that there was a gap of four months between the first interview and the second and that her new hair colour was in preparation for the start of the tour. She agreed that I could use the first interview.

On the day of the first show, we filmed some of the dress rehearsal, just a few hours before they were due to perform in front of an audience for the first time in nine years. It had been just four weeks since we had filmed them in rehearsal and I couldn't believe how much they had improved but there still seemed to be a few rough edges. I grabbed a final interview with them all together just five minutes before they were due to walk out on stage. I couldn't believe how relaxed they all seemed. Five minutes later, they were on. The place went ballistic. I got goose bumps and it was the closest thing to Beatlemania I would ever witness. I couldn't believe that they had actually pulled it off. For those ninety minutes that they were on stage, they were absolutely brilliant.

More than any other group that I have worked with aside from the Beatles, they are the ones about whom I most often get asked the question: 'what were they like?' I never got close enough to any of them to pass judgement but it was a great experience working with them and a tonic to spend time in their company. They had a great energy and did seem to believe in the whole 'girl power' ethos. I wouldn't go as far as to say they were the greatest musicians in the world; for them it was never about that, but collectively they had that thing that all great groups have. The whole was much greater than the sum of its parts and they definitely deserve their place in the pantheon of great British pop bands.

NO TALKING HEADS

My fears that my credibility would be damaged by working with what was considered a 'pop act' proved to be unfounded. The following year, I was back working with the Beatles. Jonathan Clyde at Apple got in touch to say that they had just finished re-mastering the back catalogue of all their albums and for the first time ever these were going to be made available via download on iTunes. The release of each album was going to be accompanied by a ten-minute documentary. Jonathan asked if I would be interested in putting these documentaries together. The only stipulation was that we would not be filming any interviews with the Beatles; they would be represented in film and audio archive. I would have access to every interview they had given either on film or tape during the past fifty years. It would almost be like making a radio programme, to which we would then add the visuals to complement the audio. This was a great idea and something that to my knowledge had never been attempted before.

We made thirteen short documentaries, ranging from between eight and ten minutes long; one for each of the albums that were being re-released. Jonathan then asked if I thought we might be able to compile the mini documentaries in such a way that we could make a one-hour standalone film. We did this and it was broadcast on BBC2 as *The Beatles on Record*. The documentary was nominated for an Emmy. My editor Julian Caidan and I, along with Jonathan Clyde, went to New York for the ceremony. On this occasion, we didn't get to pick up the award but just the fact that we had been nominated proved that the idea of not shooting any talking head interviews had worked.

I would use a similar technique when we eventually got around to making the feature-length Jimi Hendrix film that I had been discussing with John McDermott for a number of years. John now had a title for the film: Voodoo Child. He had also decided that he wanted the story to be told in Jimi's own words. Over the past three years, John had been pulling together every interview that Jimi had ever given during his short life. These interviews had all been transcribed and John gave them to me saying that they would form the basis for the narrative of the film. I spent the next three months editing the document down on paper, into a complete narrative of Jimi's life told in the first person. We had the script. Now we just needed someone to be the voice of Jimi.

Janie Hendrix suggested Bootsy Collins, who had been the bass player in Funkadelic and had also played with James Brown. His credentials as a musician were unquestionable but how he would fair with regards to doing the voice, I didn't have a clue. Bootsy had never done anything like this before but Janie had met him and thought he had a good vibe about him, and that he sounded a bit like Jimi.

I emailed Bootsy to introduce myself and said that I would send him a section of the script and for him to record himself reading it and get it back to me. The next day, an audio file dropped into my inbox with the recording of Bootsy reading the script. It was like the worst Jimi Hendrix impersonator I had ever heard in my life. I thought the least I could do was call him and thank him for his efforts, and break the news to him that this wasn't going to work. When I put the call through and he answered the phone and I heard his normal speaking voice, I was shocked. He did sound like Jimi. I thanked him for sending the recording and asked if he could do it again but this time read it in his own voice; not to try and sound like Jimi. Half an hour later, another recording arrived. It wasn't perfect but I thought that we might have something that could work.

Bootsy told me he was going to be in Miami later that month, watching his team the Indianapolis Colts play in the final of the Super

Bowl, and that he would be able to do the recording while he was there. I turned up at Bootsy's hotel to meet him for the first time, to take him to the studio. Now, if you have never seen any footage or photographs of Bootsy, go on line and have a look. Put it this way: as well as being famous for his bass-playing, he was almost as famous for his extravagant stage outfits. When he came down to meet me in the reception of the hotel, he was dressed like he was just about to go on stage at the Apollo in New York, not to spend a day in the studio. But I was impressed that he had dressed for the occasion. Bootsy shook my hand and said, "Pleased to meet you, Bob, I like your outfit." I must admit, I felt a bit underdressed in my shorts, flip-flops and t-shirt.

We had booked the studio for a full day to record sixty pages of script which amounted to around one hour of narrative. Before we got started, Bootsy told me how much he loved Jimi, that he felt privileged to be doing this; he wanted to do a good job and was prepared to work really hard until he got it right. After around two hours we had recorded two lines. Not only was Bootsy struggling with the reading, he was putting in words that were not in the script and, on occasion, that were not even in the English language. He was well out of his comfort zone and I would have totally understood if he had decided to throw the towel in. But it was obvious how much he wanted to make this work and he never lost his sense of humour, even when I had to keep telling him that he wasn't getting it right.

John called at the end of the day and asked me how it was going. I explained to him that Bootsy was doing really well but we had only recorded the first three pages of the script and that he best book us in the studio for another two days. By the middle of the second day, Bootsy had learned how to take direction and was going great guns but there would still be the odd occasion when he put in an invented word and we would both be on the floor laughing. After three days, he had read the whole of the script.

Julian Caidan and I were in stitches when we started listening back to the recordings. We had around five hours of various takes that we had to listen to and assemble into a script. Eventually, after around two weeks of surreptitious editing, we had the hour of narrative that we needed. We then lowered the pitch of Bootsy's voice, to put it in the same register as Jimi's. Julian and I sat back and listened to Bootsy as the voice of Jimi. It sounded great. In essence, we now had a one-hour radio show. The next stage was to lay in the music and the pictures, in the same way that we had done with *The Beatles on Record*.

We opened the film with a scrapbook that bore the title: *Jimi Hendrix Voodoo Child*. When the scrapbook was opened to reveal a photograph of Jimi as a baby, we began our first line of our 'Bootsy as Jimi' dialogue. "I was born in Seattle, Washington, USA, on November 27th 1942, at the age of zero."

The effect was of Jimi telling us his story as he looked back at his life through the scrapbook, which contained photographs, personal letters, artefacts and archive footage. We hadn't gone down the well-trodden path of interviewing people that knew Jimi or had an opinion on him; there were no talking heads.

YOU MAKE ME WANNA SHOUT

Every Friday, as I had done for over twenty years, I would head back home to Newcastle. But it was getting harder to rally my mates for a night out. It would appear that a night on the Quayside was not as good a proposition as it had been twenty years ago. And once I had been over to Benwell to spend a couple of hours with my mam, I would often find myself spending the rest of the weekend on my own in the house where Karen and I had lived for five of the fifteen years that we had been together.

I now had a bunch of mates in London; Mo, Drew, JB, and Jake who owned the Wellington, a private members' club in Knightsbridge. They couldn't understand why I was never in the club on a Friday or Saturday night.

I still had my platinum club ticket at St James' so that was one reason to head back home but since the club had been bought by Mike Ashley – a Cockney businessman – things were not looking good for the Toon.

I had also started seeing an Australian girl called Linda, who also worked in television and had been living in London for fifteen years. On the odd occasion, I would stay down and spend the weekend with her. I discovered that London at the weekend had a lot going for it.

Eventually, I did something that I had always promised myself I would never do. I moved to London. I could never totally cut my ties with Newcastle, and would still go back every couple of months to see my mam and my brother and sister, and catch up with my mates, but

I no longer travelled back religiously on a Friday night. As Bob Dylan had once remarked, the times were changing. But what I realised was that you carry home inside of you no matter where you are and you only change the person you are if you want to change.

I had put in a proposal to Pete Townshend with a view to making a film about the Who's *Quadrophenia* album. Another director had also put in a proposal, so it was going to come down to me or this other guy as to who would get to make the film. As I had worked with Pete in the past, I felt that this would work in my favour. Sure enough, Pete looked at both of the proposals and went for the one that I had written. We set a date for when we were going to start shooting, then Pete came back and said he would have to delay the filming for around three months as he was tied up with writing his autobiography. I thought, great, I could sit back and relax, knowing that in three months I would be working with the Who again. Then the BBC, who were going to broadcast the film, got in touch and said while I was waiting on Townshend to become available they had something else that they thought I might be up for doing: a documentary on Lulu.

They wanted the film to run for ninety minutes and would like it to be ready for broadcast in ten weeks. To turn a ninety-minute film around in ten weeks would be really pushing it and to make a film of that length would require a lot of material. It would need to have an angle besides being a straightforward biography of Lulu. I told the BBC of my concerns but they were adamant; Lulu was a 'national treasure', everyone loved her and they had decided she was worthy of a feature-length film. My instinct told me to say no to the job; I had been working with some of the biggest names in music and I never lost sight of how lucky I was. It might sound like a cliché but, while it was great to be paid for something that I loved doing, money was never my motivation.

I did something else that I said I would never do. I took a job just for the money.

I went along and met Lulu and her manager, to see if there was an angle on the film. During the course of our chat, Lulu mentioned in passing that when she had her first hit with *Shout* back in 1965 she was only fifteen and had no control over the direction her career was taking, and had subsequently been side-tracked into the world of 'light entertainment'. She went on to say that she wished that she had stuck to the path she had started out on when she was a kid growing up in Glasgow, to be acknowledged as a great singer, and that was going to be her goal from here on in.

I had my angle. I would tell Lulu's story from the perspective of someone who had tasted fame at an early age and had drifted into light entertainment but who now, at the age of sixty-three, was looking to re-establish herself as a great singer.

As luck would have it, she was just about to start rehearsals with her band for an upcoming UK tour, and the final gig was going to be in Glasgow.

The first thing I filmed was Lulu in rehearsal with the band. I had always rated her as a singer but had maybe underestimated how good she really was. One of the songs she sang was the Otis Redding classic, *Try a Little Tenderness*. She totally nailed it. I had a feeling this strand of the film would work and, when tied in with the biographical elements, give me a solid grounding for the film.

Lulu had given me a big list of her showbiz pals who she felt would have a comment or two about her. Gary Barlow, who she had sung a duet with in his Take That days, was not available. Neither was Barry Gibb of the Bee Gees, whose brother Maurice she had been married to. But we would get to interview the other brother, Robin, along with Cliff Richard, Kylie Minogue, and Elton John.

The person I was most looking forward to interviewing was soul legend Bobby Womack. Bobby had recorded a duet with Lulu back in the early 1990s and just happened to be in London for a gig at the Jazz Café in Camden Town.

On the day we were due to interview Bobby, Barry Manilow was also in town, for a gig at the O2 Arena, and had also agreed to sit for an interview. Bobby Womack and Barry Manilow on the same day; this was going to be a turn up for the books.

I arrived to interview Barry Manilow at the Strand Hotel and, as would be expected of a star of his stature, he had a whole host of his people present. I was told not to sit too close to Barry as this made him uncomfortable and that I would only be allowed five minutes of his time.

When I started the interview, I was sat around six feet away from Barry and I asked if he minded if I pulled my chair closer to him as I didn't want to have to shout my questions. Barry told me, "Come as close as you like." After five minutes, I told him we had to stop there as my time was up. He said, "Take as long as you need, I love Lulu and I'm really enjoying this." Within around fifteen minutes, I had pretty much covered all of my questions. I thanked Barry and headed off to interview Bobby Womack.

Bobby was staying at the Holiday Inn in Kilburn and when we arrived he was sat alone in his room watching daytime television. Unlike Barry, he wasn't surrounded by an entourage. In my eyes this guy was a true genius; not only was he one of the greatest soul singers of all time but he had written a number of classic songs, including *It's All Over Now*, which had given the Rolling Stones their first-ever UK number one.

I began the interview by asking him, "Bobby, when did you first become aware of Lulu?"

Bobby replied, "I heard this voice on the radio and I just loved it and I knew this was a great singer."

I then asked, "Could you tell me what is your favourite song of Lulu's and why it resonates with you?"

He answered, "I love all of Lulu's songs. It would be hard just to pick one, they all mean so much to me."

I followed up with, "Can you tell me how you and Lulu came to work together?"

Bobby replied, "You know, I have been lucky to work with some great singers during my career and Lulu was another one of those."

Then Bobby said, "Do you mind if I ask you a question, who is this Lulu that you keep asking me about?"

I couldn't believe he had done the interview without having any idea who Lulu was, and when I showed him a clip of them singing together on *Top of the Pops*, he couldn't recall ever working with her. Even though he had no recollection of Lulu, he was a real pro and he still gave me answers that I was able to use when I was assembling the documentary. Bobby Womack was a true legend and the short time I spent in his company turned out to be my happiest memory of making the Lulu film.

There is always a certain amount of anxiety at the start of any project but once you have your first four of five 'shoot days' under your belt, you usually begin to feel confident that things are taking shape, and start to relax. On this occasion, I had pretty much done all of my filming but I was worried that I didn't have the material I needed. The footage we had shot with Lulu and her band had worked really well, and the homecoming gig that we filmed – though not quite Glastonbury – would provide the ending that I had imagined for the film.

The problem was, I was not getting the material I needed from Lulu during our interview set-ups. I got the impression that she was reluctant to re-visit certain parts of her life. She was happy to talk about her range of skin-care products that she would promote on the QVC television channel but there was reluctance to let me get the material about her personal life. This was a woman who had lived almost fifty years in the showbiz spotlight, been married twice – once to a Bee Gee and once to celebrity hairdresser John Frieda – and had an alleged fling with David Bowie. I felt like I was getting a sanitised version of her story.

It takes a lot of people to make a film and I have been fortunate to work with some great producers, cameramen, sound recordists, editors, archive researchers, production managers and runners. But at the end of the day, the buck stops with the director; when it all goes great it's the director who gets the glory but if there is a fuck-up, it's the director who takes the shit. Now here I was, on what I had thought was going to be a straightforward biography that was pushing me to the edge. I would go to bed at midnight and wake up again at two a.m., and not be able to get back to sleep until six a.m. and then be up at seven a.m. I was drained and couldn't think straight. I promised myself that I would never again take a job just for the money.

To add insult to injury, I had four weeks left on the project when Pete Townshend got in touch and said he now had a window in his schedule and was ready to begin filming the *Quadrophenia* documentary. He was unable to wait for me to finish the Lulu doc and the job went to another director. I was close to tears.

I asked the production company if the BBC would take a one-hour version of the film. I was told that they had commissioned a ninety-minute film so that was what I had to deliver. I had a cut that ran for eighty minutes. I enlisted the help of my old pal, Jools Holland, who Lulu had toured with, and he agreed to do a song at the piano with her. Former Spice Girl Melanie Chisholm helped me out, and the couple of quotes she gave me added to my running time. Eventually, I had a cut of the film that was ninety minutes long. We showed it to the BBC and they were happy with it.

I felt that I had fulfilled my remit and the finished film showed how Lulu was now intent on proving to the world that she was a great singer.

Three weeks before the documentary was screened, it was announced that Lulu had agreed to take part in *Strictly Come Dancing*, the BBC's highest-rated 'light entertainment' show.

A couple of months after the documentary was broadcast, I was walking with Linda and our dog Archie through Hyde Park. I bumped into Lulu, who was walking her dog. We kissed each other on the cheek and were both very pleasant with each other. That's Showbiz, folks!!

'HEAR MY TRAIN A COMIN'

I was surprised when John McDermott said he wanted to make another Hendrix film. I thought that we pretty much had the last word on Jimi's life when we made the *Voodoo Child* film but John had other ideas. He showed me a clip that had never been seen before, of Jimi at the Miami Pop Festival 1968. The footage was fantastic; it was in colour and showed Jimi in all his glory during a period when he was at the peak of his powers. John wanted to make a ninety-minute film built around Jimi's performance at the festival. As great as the footage was, I felt there wasn't the back story to accompany it. I had been burnt by the Lulu experience and didn't want to be caught out with not enough material to warrant a ninety-minute film.

Then PBS, the American broadcaster, got in touch and said they would like to make a film about Hendrix as part of their flagship *American Masters* series. Their stipulations were that they wanted Jimi's story from birth to death, and they also wanted to bring on board an American director. John told them I was 'his guy' and that if I wasn't allowed to make the film, there would be no film.

What was originally intended to be a film about Jimi's concert in Miami became another telling of the 'Jimi Hendrix Story', this time with talking heads and all that this type of documentary would entail. The one difference would be that we hoped to get a number of people who had never done so previously to talk on film about Jimi. John was convinced that he would be able to get Jimi's former girlfriends to talk about Jimi the man, rather than the 'genius guitarist and musician'; we hoped that angle would be addressed by the likes of Paul McCartney and Bob Dylan.

John was able to secure us interviews with three of Jimi's girlfriends and they, as we had hoped, gave us an insight into his personality. Jimi, they said, was a very different man off stage to on; rather than being super-confident and flash, he was in fact quite shy. But what was undeniable was that women found him irresistible and he took full advantage of that, even before he became 'Jimi Hendrix - Rock Star'.

I also got to interview Paul McCartney, who didn't normally do this type of thing. I am sure that our shared history had something to do with him agreeing to be interviewed. Paul told me how he helped secure Jimi a slot at the Monterey Pop Festival back in 1967 and that the promoters of that festival had originally wanted the Beatles to appear. Paul had told them that the Beatles were never going to perform live again, but suggested booking this great guitarist that he had seen playing around the clubs in London.

The Jimi Hendrix Experience made their US debut at Monterey. The rest, as they say, is history. It was obvious that Paul was a massive fan of Hendrix and the people at American Masters were delighted that we had been able to secure an interview with him. Now we had to try and get Dylan.

John McDermott had been in touch with Bob Dylan's manager and was told that there was a good possibility that Bob would talk on film about Hendrix. Since I had started listening to Dylan back in '97 there wasn't a week that went by when I would not listen to him. Aside from meeting Elvis Presley, which was never going to happen, the one guy I said I would love to meet was Dylan. Just to walk up to him and say, "Hi Bob, I'm Bob" would have be one of the highlights of my life.

We were filming in Los Angeles and Bob lived just down the road in Malibu. His manager came back to us and said that Bob had requested that we show him four questions we would like to ask him; Bob would then decide if he would do an interview. I had to remind myself that the questions I was going to ask him had to do with Jimi Hendrix, otherwise I wouldn't know where to begin. I wrote out my four questions. These went off to Bob and the next day his manager told us that Bob had read my questions and was up for doing the interview.

When the day came around, his manager came back and said something had come up and he was not going to be able to do the interview on that day. I was bitterly disappointed but to think that Bob had read something that I had written gave me some measure of comfort. Throughout the process of putting the film together, I was hoping that the phone would ring to tell me that Bob was now available but sadly that call never came.

Despite my initial reservations that we were covering old ground in making this film, with the interviews that John had been able to secure and the unseen footage, we were able to put together a film that I felt gave a different insight into Jimi Hendrix than had been seen in previous films. I flew to New York to show a 98-minute cut to the people at PBS for their feedback and suggestions as to which eight minutes I should lose to bring it in at 90 minutes.

I returned to London and, along with my editor, Stephen Ellis, started cutting the film to length and making the additions that PBS had requested. Then I got a call to say the film had to run for two hours. I couldn't believe it; I thought the film was too long at 98 minutes and that it would benefit by being shorter but now I was being told to extend it by over twenty minutes. I was furious and threatened to resign but it was suggested that I take the emotion out of the situation and just get on with extending the film.

I found it hard to take the emotion out of the situation. I had put over a year of my life into this project and felt strongly that the film was too long. But John McDermott had always been good to me and had insisted that I make the documentary when PBS had wanted to have one of their directors make the film. I extended the film as requested.

I did in fact make a ninety-minute cut, which was broadcast on the BBC, and an additional cut of the same length for PBS, which they showed at a later date as the Director's Cut. Apparently it was the first time a 'director's cut' had ever been shorter than the original version.

PBS really went to town promoting the film and had me over to the States to appear on *Good Morning America*, which was broadcast to over five million people. I did a whole load of other television and radio press to promote the film and, in general, *Hear My Train A Comin'* was well received. It went on to win an Emmy Award.

While I was in LA, we also screened the film to an invited audience at the Grammy museum and afterwards John McDermott and I did a question-and-answer session. As we were nearing the end of the session, a guy put up his hand and asked, "Are you the Bob Smeaton that used to be in White Heat?" I couldn't believe it; here I was, over thirty years after the band had broken up, and I was still 'Bob Smeaton that used to be in White Heat'.

I said, "Yes, I am that Bob Smeaton, and being in that band was the greatest thing that I have ever done. If I had not spent the time in the band, I would not be sitting here now."

A MEETING WITH THE MODFATHER

When *Festival Express* was shown at the Miami Film Festival back in 2004, it was the only music documentary in the festival. Ten years later, music documentaries had become the 'big thing'; there were film festivals that would show nothing but music documentaries.

When I was invited to attend a screening of *Hear My Train A Comin'* at the In-Edit music documentary festival being held in Sao Paulo, the guy who was organising the festival told me that he had received 400 submissions from people wanting to show their films in the festival. Bands who had not even released their first album, and artists who had been just a footnote in music history, were being given the documentary feature treatment. I was flattered to be invited along but Brazil was a long way to travel to spend a couple of hours watching the film, only to jump back on a plane twenty-four hours later. I told the guy organising the festival that I would let him know.

One band who hadn't as yet been the subject of a retrospective were the Jam. The Sex Pistols and the Clash, who along with the Jam had been at the forefront of the punk rock explosion in the mid-1970s, had each had a couple of films made about them but so far the Jam had resisted the temptation. The reason for this, so I had heard, was that Paul Weller – the frontman, vocalist and main songwriter – was a mod, and part of the ethos of being a mod was that he did not like 'looking back'. With this in mind, I was surprised when my mate, the radio DJ Gary Crowley, asked me if I would be interested in making a film about the Jam. The first thing I asked Gary was, "Is Weller on board?"

Gary said, "I think he could be if we make the focus of the film not just about the band but also about the fans."

The first decision I had to make before meeting Weller was what to wear. Now, this wouldn't normally be a consideration prior to meeting someone about a potential film, but Weller was the 'Modfather', and remains one of the sharpest-dressed blokes in music. I didn't want to blow my chances of making the doc by turning up wearing the wrong sort of shoes. So when I pitched up and knocked on Weller's front door, I had dug out my old desert boots, my Fred Perry t-shirt, and in the trouser department I was wearing the closest thing in my wardrobe to a pair of Levi Sta Prest. I might not have passed for a mod back in Brighton in the summer of 1964 but in Queen's Park in the spring of 2014 I thought that I would just about pass muster.

I was feeling a bit nervous as he had a reputation for being a bit difficult but I hoped that when he saw that I was a fellow mod, he might go easy on me. He opened his door wearing a pair of cut-off Levi jeans, a blue vest, and a pair of flip-flops. He must have been relaxing that day but he still looked super-cool. I must have looked like a right twat.

I sat in Paul's back garden with his sister Nicky, and Gary Crowley, while Paul put the kettle on and made us all a cup of tea. The first question Paul asked me was, "When you did *The Beatles Anthology* and you interviewed McCartney on the boat, where was the boat?" He then proceeded to quote lines of dialogue that were used in the *Anthology* that even I had forgotten. He is a massive Beatles fan and I am sure would have happily spent the next couple of hours talking about nothing else. Eventually, I was able to steer the conversation around to the possibility of doing a documentary about his own band.

It was obvious that he was going to be uncomfortable if the focus of the film was purely about the Jam, but seemed into the idea that part of the focus would be the effect that the band had on their legions of, mainly working class, fans, and how they had been the inspiration for a great many of those fans to rise above what was expected of them once they left school and went out into the world. I told him that when

I had seen the Jam back in 1977 I had thought that if he could make it, coming from his background, there was no reason that someone like me couldn't do the same. He seemed to be warming to the idea.

Before we got up to leave, I gave him my usual spiel that if he agreed to us making the documentary this would be 'his film' and it would only be as good as he allowed it to be. He told me, "It's not my fucking film, mate, it's yours." He wasn't going to fall for my tried and tested line. When I left Paul's house, I had no idea if I would ever get to make a documentary about the Jam.

BRAZIL 2014

While I was waiting to hear what Weller would decide, my girlfriend suggested that I accept the invitation to attend the screening of *Hear My Train A Comin'* at the In-Edit Film Festival in Sao Paulo. She pointed out that I had never been to Brazil before and it was just before the World Cup so I would be able to soak up some of the atmosphere, and there were worse places to spend a weekend. I convinced myself that I should go and thought that, rather than travel straight back, I would go to Rio and spend a few days there. I had always wanted to go a for a run along the famous boardwalk along Copacabana beach and this was my chance to do so.

After watching the film, I caught a flight up to Rio and the first thing I did when I got into the hotel was put on my running gear and go for that run. It was pissing down with rain but I thought that, if for no other reason, the trip was worthwhile.

The next morning when I woke up, it was still grey and overcast so I knew I would not be hanging out on the beach. I went online and Googled 'things to do in Rio'. One of the suggestions was a two-hour hike up a mountain called Pedra da Gàvea. I thought I could handle that.

I jumped into a cab outside of the hotel and asked to be deposited at the bottom of Pedra da Gàvea. I stood on the shore and looked up towards the top of the mountain. It seemed miles away, and I started thinking that it might take longer than two hours to get up there. In fact, after walking for almost two hours, I was in the middle of what seemed like a tropical jungle. I hadn't realised that the hike would take me through this sort of terrain and I wasn't really dressed appropriately, in my trainers, t-shirt and shorts. Another oversight on my behalf was that I had not brought any water. I soldiered on for another hour or so yet still seemed to be no nearer to the top. I realised that no one knew where I was, I had no phone signal, it was hot as all hell, and I was starting to feel a bit dizzy and a little bit scared. But I convinced myself that pretty soon I would reach the top. I continued upwards.

The further I climbed, the darker it became. At one point, a monkey crossed my path and I nearly shit myself, and then some crazy-looking multi-coloured bird with goggle eyes popped its head out of the bush and squawked at me. Maybe I was hallucinating due to the heat and lack of water. I must have been climbing that bloody mountain for close to four hours. I looked at my watch and made the decision that if I had not reached the top within the next half-hour, I was going to turn around and head back. Twenty minutes later, I walked out of the foliage onto the plateau at the top of the mountain. It was beautiful.

I was actually in the clouds. I couldn't have climbed any higher. I looked down and I could see the foot of the mountain, where I had started my journey. I felt a great sense of achievement. I hadn't given up, I had kept moving forward, and I had reached the top of the mountain.

That evening, feeling slightly delirious after my exertions, I sat on Copacabana Beach, watched the sun setting behind Pedra da Gàvea, and reflected on my climb up the mountain. I started to think that maybe it was a metaphor for life. You begin your journey not knowing what lies ahead or how hard it might get. When things get tough, you keep driving yourself onwards. Finally, you reach the point where you stop, reflect on your journey, and give yourself a pat on the back for having made it this far.

A couple of months before flying out to Brazil, my friend Andy Matthews, the editor on *The Beatles Anthology*, had died. Chips

Chipperfield, who had produced the series and had become one of my best friends, had died in 2008, just a few months after Neil Aspinall. Back in 1997, when I had attended the funeral of Derek Taylor, I spoke to George Harrison for the very last time. Four years later, George also passed away.

George was a wise old soul and I remembered him telling me back in 1994 that one day I would write a book about the Beatles. Working on the *Anthology* had been a high point of my life. Now here I was twenty years later. Maybe it was the right time to reflect on that period; also on the road that had taken me to the foot of that metaphorical mountain and how, when I reached the peak, I had looked for new mountains to climb.

I started writing my book on the flight back home from Brazil. I knew it would start with me collecting my Grammy on stage at Madison Square Garden; I had pretty much written that by the time I touched down at Heathrow. I also knew that the final chapter and cut-off point would be my climb up the mountain and recent meeting with Paul Weller. People would be able to Google 'Bob Smeaton Jam Documentary' to see if I ever got around to making it; if not, it would have been another one of those that died on the vine.

I had my beginning and my end, now all I had to do was fill in the middle.

SYDNEY, AUSTRALIA, JANUARY 2018

It took me almost four years to fill in the middle bit. In the period between climbing that mountain in Brazil and now, whenever I wasn't working on a documentary I would get back to writing. I approached telling my story in the same way that I would have if I was telling someone else's. I did all of my research, started making a time-line of events, then made notes on the bits that I thought were interesting. I was fortunate in doing my research that I had diaries that went back as far as the mid-1980s. It was strange reading those diaries; I noticed how little I had really changed. The things I worried about then are the same things I worry about now. I noticed the desire to keep moving forward, along with the fear of having nothing to do. Looking back, I also realised that in both my professional and personal life I have often been overly judgemental of those closest to me. Even when they were giving their best, at times this was never good enough. This has been a failing of mine and something that I regret.

I did at one point start speaking to people that I knew in order to try and fill in some gaps in my story, but their memories didn't always tally with mine. When we were doing *The Beatles Anthology*, Neil Aspinall used to say that everyone saw things differently, even when they were all sitting in the same room, because everyone sees things from their own perspective. There were many other people who were 'in the room' and their recollections might differ from mine, but this was my story and I wanted to tell it how I saw it.

During 2016, my girlfriend Linda was offered a job 'back home'. She asked if I would consider moving to Sydney on the understanding that if it didn't work out we could always come back to the UK. I was up for a change of scenery and said, "Yeah, let's go for it."

Before leaving the UK, I went up to see my mam in Newcastle and told her that I was going to be spending some time in Australia, but not to worry and that we would stay in touch by phone. I had taken my Grammys along with me and asked her if she would take care of them for me while I was away. When I put them on top of her telly, she asked me what they were. When I told her, she said they looked very nice.

Not long after arriving in Australia, thanks to Facebook I caught up with an old mate of mine, Mick Attridge, who was now living in Sydney. Mick and I had not seen each other for almost 35 years and as we sat having a couple of beers outside the Bondi Hotel on Bondi Beach, we soon began reminiscing about the old days, when we were both working in the shipyards in Wallsend before taking our redundancy. Mick commented on how we were lucky to have made it out when we did. He went on to say how he had a recurring dream where he is back in the yards, telling his mates that he is only back temporarily and that he will be leaving again soon. I told Mick that I have had the exact same dream, and I think it's to remind us not to forget where we came from.

Sydney is eleven hours ahead of the UK and one morning I was up at 2am to watch Newcastle play against Crystal Palace at St James' Park. (We won 1-0.) During the game, the camera panned across the crowd to Sting and Jimmy Nail. The commentator said, "Sat on the right is North East legend Sting and, next to him, Jimmy Nail."

This made me laugh and got me thinking about the time back in 1979 when Jimmy came on stage with the intention of throttling me, when I was beginning to think that being in a band might just be my passport out of the shipyards. And it was Sting whose picture I had on the wall of my flat in Benwell, who had been the inspiration to start keeping the diaries that would subsequently prove so useful in my research when writing this book.

Last weekend, Paul Weller was playing a show at the Opera House. Walking up towards that iconic venue on a beautiful summer evening, I got quite emotional when I realised it had been just over forty years since I had seen Weller fronting the Jam at the Mayfair in Newcastle. I was as excited at seeing a live band as I had been back then. Before the gig started, I could hear the buzz of the amplifiers and hiss of the PA system and my guts started to churn with excitement. I still remember what it felt like to walk out on a stage; it remains the best feeling in the world.

When I told my friend Martin Smith that I was writing a memoir, he suggested a good title: *A Charmed Life*. In a way this is true, but it has had its ups and downs. The bottle of Dom Perignon that I was given by George Harrison back in 1995 still sits unopened in my kitchen cupboard as Newcastle have yet to win a major trophy, and there has been no baby's head to wet.

As I sit here writing these final few paragraphs, I have a view of the Sydney Harbour Bridge. The resemblance that it has to the bridge that crosses the River Tyne has not escaped my attention. In terms of miles, I couldn't be further away from Newcastle, but I have never felt closer to the place.

My story began on the banks of the Tyne and deep down in my heart I have a feeling that it will end there; and you know what? I guess I have had a 'charmed life'.

ACKNOWLEDGEMENTS

Thanks to Ian Snowball and to my friends in Australia, Jac Archer, Pattie Roberts, Ros Brusasco and Alan Hornsby who knew nothing about my story but upon reading my 'work in progress' thought it was worth telling. I would also like to thank Susan Lowndes and Andrew Cowell for providing me with a great place to work and live in Sydney.

Special thanks to all the people who I have met along the way who have not been mentioned in this book (they know who they are) who have given me encouragement and support in all of my various endeavours and were instrumental in giving me something to write about.

Jamie Rugge-Price introduced me to Katharine Smith who provided invaluable guidance in helping to shape this book beyond a first draft that would have given *War and Peace* a run for its money.

Special thanks to my 'pack mates' Linda and Archie for their support and for the adventures we have shared.

Printed in Great Britain
by Amazon

38512944R00162